Praise for *Afterburn*

With rare insight, clarity, and compassion, Richard Heinberg helps us face the music. Over the years, since *The Party's Over*, his books have earned our trust with their accuracy in delineating the limits of the possible. Now in this bold collection of essays, he helps us see the landscape being bequeathed us by the Great Burning — an understanding that is necessary to the Great Turning — and will save us considerable time and confusion. With ever more gratitude I bow to those who shake us awake.

—Joanna Macy, author, *Coming Back to Life:
The Updated Guide to the Work That Reconnects.*

Afterburn gives us a sense of a survivable future – hope fed by Heinberg's realistic deeper analysis, a sense of the trends ahead, and a bold (largely local) plan. Few are as good at the craft of synthesizing this powerful package then Richard Heinberg. This book will help fuel the future.

—Randy Hayes, Rainforest Action Network Founder
& Director of Foundation Earth

In my business we have a saying: hope is a terrible investment strategy. Let's go further and say hope alone is a terrible strategy, period. Yet most of society continues to simply ignore the freely available and terribly important information about where we are headed on this planet, and simply hope that things will work themselves out somehow. They won't, and we all know that now on some level. *Afterburn* bravely and thoughtfully examines the predicament we face, one idea and one fact at a time. Those who can stir in a few facts along with their hope will be able to both understand and foresee what the future holds. Pick up this book. Read it. Discuss it. Let it sink into your bones, and then understand that this book is not asking you to abandon hope, it is inviting us all to greatness.

—Chris Martenson, PhD, Co-founder of Peak Prosperity

Afterburn is like a "Richard Heinberg's Greatest Hits" compilation, drawing together a selection of his prolific output from the last few years. To choose what went in must have been to pore over an embarrassment of riches, given his seemingly untiring creativity and brilliance. He writes with incision, with passion, with rage, with compassion, and *Afterburn* captures in one single publication why he's such a shining light of insight in times of much darkness. *The Party's Over* changed my life. Perhaps *Afterburn* will change yours.

—Rob Hopkins, founder, Transition Town movement
and author, *The Power of Just Doing Stuff*

AFTERBURN

AFTERBURN

SOCIETY BEYOND FOSSIL FUELS

RICHARD HEINBERG

new society
PUBLISHERS

Cover design by Diane McIntosh.
Background texture: (image #44848082 Ess) C iStock propeller;
Flames: (image #18007634 Ess) C iStock -M-I-S-H-A-(Essentials Collection)

Printed in Canada. First printing January 2015.

New Society Publishers acknowledges the financial support of the Government of Canada
through the Canada Book Fund (CBF) for our publishing activities.

Inquiries regarding requests to reprint all or part of *Afterburn*
should be addressed to New Society Publishers at the address below.

To order directly from the publishers, please call toll-free
(North America) 1-800-567-6772, or order online at www.newsociety.com

Any other inquiries can be directed by mail to:

New Society Publishers
P.O. Box 189, Gabriola Island, BC V0R 1X0, Canada
(250) 247-9737

LIBRARY AND ARCHIVES CANADA CATALOGUING IN PUBLICATION

Heinberg, Richard, author
Afterburn : society beyond fossil fuels / Richard Heinberg.

A collection of 15 essays written in the years 2011–2014 and previously
published on the websites resilience.org, commondreams.org, and
earthisland.org, and in Orion magazine.

Includes bibliographical references and index.
Issued in print and electronic formats.
ISBN 978-0-86571-788-6 (pbk.). — ISBN 978-1-55092-584-5 (ebook)

1. Social ecology. 2. Economic development—Environmental aspects.
3. Economic development—Social aspects. 4. Social change. I. Title.

HM681.H44 2015   304.2   C2014-906816-6
                                       C2014-906817-4

New Society Publishers' mission is to publish books that contribute in fundamental ways to building an ecologically sustainable and just society, and to do so with the least possible impact on the environment, in a manner that models this vision. We are committed to doing this not just through education, but through action. The interior pages of our bound books are printed on Forest Stewardship Council®-registered acid-free paper that is 100% post-consumer recycled (100% old growth forest-free), processed chlorine-free, and printed with vegetable-based, low-VOC inks, with covers produced using FSC®-registered stock. New Society also works to reduce its carbon footprint, and purchases carbon offsets based on an annual audit to ensure a carbon neutral footprint. For further information, or to browse our full list of books and purchase securely, visit our website at: www.newsociety.com

 **new society** PUBLISHERS

Contents

Acknowledgments

Thanks to Scott Steedman for copy editing the manuscript of *Afterburn* and to Ingrid Witvoet of New Society Publishers for shepherding this project through the publication process.

My appreciation also goes out to my colleagues Asher Miller, Daniel Lerch, and Ken White of Post Carbon Institute, who offered valuable suggestions on each of the chapters. Our conversations often spark ideas that grow to become essays and even books.

Finally, once again (as with previous books) I offer thanks to and for my wife Janet Barocco, for her support and encouragement, and for making our home a place of creativity and beauty.

▶ INTRODUCTION

WE LIVE IN THE TIME OF WHAT MIGHT BE CALLED THE GREAT Burning. However, we tend to ignore the tremendous inferno blazing around us. Most of the combustion occurs out of sight and out of mind, in hundreds of millions of automobile, truck, aircraft, and ship engines; in tens of thousands of coal- or gas-fired power plants that provide the electricity that runs our computers, smartphones, refrigerators, air conditioners, and televisions; in furnaces that warm us in the winter; in factories that spew out products we are constantly urged to buy. Add all this burning together and it amounts to the energy equivalent of torching a quarter of the Amazon rainforest every year. In the United States, the energy from annual fossil fuel combustion roughly equates to the solar energy taken up by all the biomass in the nation. It's a conflagration unlike anything that has ever occurred before in Earth's history, and it is the very basis of our modern existence.

Obviously, it would be impossible to continue consuming the world's forests, year in and year out, at a rate that far outstrips their pace of regrowth. We'd soon run out of forest. Yet the Great Burning has persisted and grown, decade after decade, because its fuel consists of millions of years' worth of stored and concentrated ancient biomass.

The burning of fossil fuels cannot go on forever, either. Coal, oil, and natural gas are depleting, nonrenewable resources—they don't grow back. While we are not about to run out of them in the absolute sense, we have extracted the cheapest and best-quality fuels first, leaving the more expensive, dirtier, and harder-to-produce fuels for the next year's takings. As I argue in the first chapter of this book, we have already reached the point of diminishing returns for investments in world oil production. And oil is the most crucial of our nonrenewable resources from an economic standpoint.

At the same time, burning Earth's vast storehouses of ancient sunlight releases carbon dioxide into the atmosphere, resulting in global warming and ocean acidification. Climate change is contributing to a mass extinction of species, extreme weather, and rising sea levels—which, taken together, could undermine the viability of civilization itself. If civilization fails, then we will have no need for cars, trucks, aircraft, ships, power plants, or furnaces—or for the oil, coal, and gas that fuel them. If the world's policy makers decide to act decisively to mitigate climate change, the result will again be a dramatic curtailment of our consumption of fossil fuels.

Thus whether due to fossil fuel depletion, environmental collapse, societal collapse, or government policy, the Great Burning will come to an end during the next few decades. If the 20th century was all about increasing our burn rate year after blazing year, the dominant trend of the 21st century will be a gradual flameout.

How shall we manage the last days of the Great Burning? And what will come next? These are quite literally the most important questions our species has ever faced.

The 15 essays collected in this book explore those questions from a variety of angles. These pieces were written in the years 2011–14 and were originally published on the websites resilience.org, commondreams.org, and earthisland.org, and in *Orion* magazine. I've organized them in a way that seems sensible, though each chapter is self-contained:

1. "Ten Years After" reviews the debate about "peak oil" from the

perspective of more than a decade's work in tracking petroleum forecasts, prices, and production numbers. As we'll see, forecasts from oil supply pessimists have turned out to be remarkably accurate, far more so than those of official energy agencies or petroleum industry spokespeople.

2. Currently, economic cheerleaders tell us that "fracking" for shale gas and tight oil will result in an ongoing energy bonanza. In "The Gross Society" I argue that this rosy forecast is supported only by cherry-picked statistics; mainstream commentators fail to mention the need for soaring rates of investment and ever-increasing rates of drilling if the promised energy supply numbers are to be realized. When we look more deeply into oil supply statistics, an entirely different reality presents itself—one of diminishing returns on the investment of money and energy in the extraction process, and the requirement for ever-more extreme and environmentally risky extraction methods.

3. Fossil fuels are all around us, powering nearly every aspect of our economy, but we rarely actually see them. "Visualize Gasoline" helps us think about how much we take for granted—in terms of both the services oil provides, and the real price we pay.

4. In "The Climate PR Puzzle" I explore why it is so difficult to craft an effective public relations message to persuade policy makers and the general public to do what is actually needed to stop global warming; I also suggest how the discussion might be reframed.

5. "The Purposely Confusing World of Energy Politics" examines the reasons for, and implications of, the remarkable state of affairs described in the following sentence: Today it is especially difficult for most people to understand our perilous global energy situation, precisely *because* it has never been more important to do so.

6. Environmentalists tend to agree that consumerism is a deal-breaking barrier to the creation of a sustainable society. It's helpful, therefore, to know exactly what consumerism is (not merely a greedy personal attitude but a system of economic organization) and how it originated (not as a natural outgrowth of "progress" but

as the deliberate creation of advertising and marketing firms). "The Brief, Tragic Reign of Consumerism" tells this story, and explores how we might go about building an alternative *sufficiency* economy.

7. Some longtime environmentalists have been anticipating global social and ecological catastrophe for many years, yet it has so far failed to manifest in all its devastating glory; what we see instead are periodic localized economic and environmental disasters from which at least partial recovery has so far been possible. "Fingers in the Dike" explains why industrial society has been able to ward off collapse for as long as it has, and suggests ways to best make use of borrowed time.

8. In 2011 a student organization at Worcester Polytechnic Institute invited me to give an alternative commencement address to the graduating class (the official commencement speaker was Rex Tillerson, CEO of ExxonMobil). "Your Post-Petroleum Future" is the text of that address.

9. "The Fight of the Century" examines four scenarios for how national leaders may try to handle the economic decline that the overdeveloped world inevitably faces.

10. Environmental philosophers are currently debating the significance of our new geological epoch, which has been dubbed the *Anthropocene* in acknowledgment of humanity's dramatically expanding impact upon Earth's natural systems. Some commentators take extreme positions, arguing the new epoch will usher in either human godhood or human extinction. "The Anthropocene: It's *Not* All About Us" suggests instead that we are about to bump against the limits of human agency and thereby regain a sense of humility in the face of natural forces beyond our control.

11. "Conflict in the Era of Economic Decline" is the text of an address to the International Conference on Sustainability, Transition and Culture Change, held in Grand Rapids, Michigan, on November 16, 2012. It discusses the kinds of social conflict we are likely to see in the decades ahead as economies contract and weather extremes worsen—including conflict between rich and poor, conflict over

dwindling resources, and conflict over access to places of refuge from natural disasters. This chapter also proposes a "post-carbon theory of change" that encourages building resilience into societal systems in order to minimize trauma from foreseeable economic and environmental stresses.

12. The notion that we're entering an era of economic decline may be depressing, but "All Roads Lead Local" offers a relatively cheerful look at the opportunities opened by the end of cheap transportation fuel. Localism is currently one of the hottest trends in the United States, and the end of globalization potentially offers loads of psychological and cultural benefits, if we are willing and able to get ahead of the trend by building local production infrastructure.

13. Historically, sustained economic booms have always (sooner or later) been followed by periods of protracted economic decline. We are just now seeing the tapering of the biggest boom in history—the fossil-fueled industrial extravaganza of the 20th century. Are we headed for a new dark age? If so, might we lose many of our scientific and technological achievements, as other societies have done under analogous conditions? "Our Evanescent Culture and the Awesome Duty of Librarians" suggests we get started now at the important task of cultural preservation.

14. "Our Cooperative Darwinian Moment" points out that, while we inevitably face a critical bottleneck of overpopulation, resource depletion, and climate change, it's up to us *how* we go through the bottleneck—whether in ruthless competition for the last scraps of natural resources, or in a burst of social innovation that brings more cooperation and sharing. Biology and history suggest the latter path is viable; it is certainly preferable. However, our chances of taking it successfully will improve to the degree that we devote much more effort now to developing cooperative institutions and attitudes.

15. Finally, advocates for social change today face a nearly unprecedented opportunity, as I argue in "Want to Change the World? Read This First." However, to make the most of it, they will need

to understand historic and current revolutionary transformations in the relationship between society and ecosystem. As society's energy systems inevitably change, we will need to reinvent our economy, our political systems, and the explicit and implicit ideologies with which we explain and justify our world. With so much at stake, there has—quite literally—never been a more crucial moment to be aware and active in helping shape the process of societal change.

Welcome to life beyond fossil fuels.

▶ TEN YEARS AFTER

I T HAS BEEN MORE THAN TEN YEARS SINCE THE PUBLICATION OF my book *The Party's Over: Oil, War and the Fate of Industrial Societies*, which has seen two editions and many printings, translations into eight languages, and sales of roughly fifty thousand copies in North America. The beginning of *The Party's Over*'s second decade has coincided with a widespread reevaluation of what has come to be known as peak oil theory (which the book helped popularize). So it's a good time to take stock of both. The following is part memoir, part reassessment, and part reflection.

Memoir: What a Party It Was

Prior to the publication of *The Party's Over* I was a writer on environmental topics and a teacher in an innovative college program on "Culture, Ecology, and Sustainable Community." In 1998, I happened to read an article in *Scientific American* titled "The End of Cheap Oil?" by two veteran petroleum geologists, Colin Campbell and Jean Laherrère.[1] At that time, oil was trading for roughly ten dollars a barrel—about the cheapest it has ever been in real terms. The article made the case that "When the world runs completely out of oil is... not directly relevant; what matters is when production begins to taper off." The commencement of that tapering, the authors said, could happen disturbingly soon: "Using several different techniques to estimate the current reserves of conventional oil and the amount still left to be discovered, we conclude that the decline will begin before 2010." History had already shown (in the 1970s) that a significant constraint to the availability of oil could have dramatic and widespread economic, financial, and political repercussions.

Around the same time, I began receiving an occasional series of emailed essays titled "Brain Food" by a retired software engineer named Jay Hanson, which discussed energy's importance in world events. I also joined an email list called EnergyResources. Hanson and others were discussing books like William Catton's *Overshoot* and Walter Youngquist's *GeoDestinies*, which I quickly devoured. As I began to recognize the central role of energy in human society, big questions I'd had about economic history—especially ones concerning the origins and significance of the Industrial Revolution—began to find answers. "The End of Cheap Oil" also led me to realize that, because humanity was on the cusp of a decline in available, cheap transport fuel, a contraction in trade and economic activity in general was fairly inevitable.

I waited for someone to write the peak oil book that would tell the story of energy, portray the politics and economics of petroleum, and lay out the world's prospects in the coming post-peak era. Surely a petroleum geologist or energy expert would step up to the plate. But none did (with the exception of Kenneth Deffeyes, whose 2001 book *Hubbert's Peak* was a bit technical and did not explain petroleum's extraordinary role in recent economic and political history). After a couple of years, I started researching the subject in earnest and put together a book proposal, which I sent to Chris and Judith Plant at New Society Publishers. They replied favorably. New Society would go on to become the foremost publisher of non-technical books in the peak oil genre, with titles by John Michael Greer, Dmitry Orlov, Sharon Astyk, and others.

The timing of the publication of *The Party's Over* proved to be pivotal: it came out in the same year the United States invaded Iraq.

In the spring of 2003, millions of Americans thronged streets in dozens of cities to protest the Bush–Cheney administration's stupid, horrific, and illegal war. Since Iraq had large, relatively untapped oil reserves, there was widespread speculation that the invasion was an exercise in trading "blood for oil." My book offered some support for this line of thought, so most of my early speaking invitations came from antiwar groups. All I had to do was remind audiences of Dick Cheney's words in a 1999 speech to the London Institute of Petroleum:

> Producing oil is obviously a self-depleting activity. Every year you've got to find and develop reserves equal to your output just to stand still, just to stay even…. By some estimates there will be an average of two percent annual growth in global oil demand over the years ahead along with conservatively a three percent natural decline in production from existing reserves. That means by 2010 we will need on the order of an additional fifty million barrels a day. So where is the oil going to come from?… [T]he Middle East, with two-thirds of the world's oil and the lowest cost, is still where the prize ultimately lies."[2]

In late 2003, I received a speaking invitation from Julian Darley and Celine Rich in Vancouver, Canada. They were in the process of organizing a local peak oil conference, and had just started a new nonprofit organization called Post Carbon Institute. They soon invited me to become a board member (and later, Senior Fellow).

The next year saw the first of several "Peak Oil and Community Solutions" conferences in Yellow Springs, Ohio (the second one was reported on at length in *Harper's*).[3] In 2004 I also attended the Association for the Study of Peak Oil (ASPO) international conference in Berlin,[4] where I met Campbell and Laherrère, Matt Simmons, and other oil experts.

The year 2005 saw speaking tours in South Africa and Britain, along with dozens more appearances in the United States. Especially memorable was a conference in Kinsale, Ireland, organized by Rob Hopkins—who immediately impressed me as someone capable of doing great things (he started the Transition Towns initiatives just a year later). That summer the *New York Times Magazine* published a long profile article about Bill Clinton, mentioning that *The Party's Over* was on his current reading list and that he had underlined many passages and scribbled comments throughout. Also that year, James Howard Kunstler published *The Long Emergency*, which introduced an even wider audience to the dilemma of oil depletion.

By 2006 it was possible to speak of a peak oil "movement": Totnes in the UK had become the world's first Transition Town; both ASPO International and ASPO USA were holding annual conferences to highlight relevant technical issues; the Arthur Morgan Institute for Community Solutions was hosting annual peak oil gatherings in Ohio for the activist crowd; several peak oil websites, including TheOilDrum.com and EnergyBulletin.net, reported brisk traffic; the list of peak oil books and peer-reviewed papers was lengthening; and a growing roster of public speakers was lecturing on the dim prospects of the oil industry and the dimmer prospects of the world's oil-dependent economies.

My personal career morphed in tandem: I moved from teaching to a full-time position with Post Carbon Institute. When I wasn't on the road speaking, I was writing more books—*Powerdown* (2004), *The Oil Depletion Protocol* (2006), *Peak Everything* (2007), *Blackout* (2009), *The End of Growth* (2011), and *Snake Oil* (2013)—as well as blogs, articles, essays, reports, and forewords to, or endorsements of, other authors' books.

Post Carbon Institute meanwhile recruited 28 fellows; compiled a *Post Carbon Reader* that is now on college curricula around the nation; published other books (including *Energy: Overdevelopment and the Delusion of Endless Growth* and the *Community Resilience Guides* series); produced award-winning video animations;[5] and commissioned several important papers and reports, including David Hughes's influential critique of US shale resources, "Drill, Baby, Drill."[6]

A thrilling decade it was. And here we are now…with press articles appearing almost daily featuring some variation of the title, "Peak Oil Is Dead." What the hell happened?

Reassessment: Was (or Is) the Party Really Over?

The central claim of many recent "Peak Oil Is Dead" articles is that peak oil theorists were simply wrong.[7] Were we? Well, let's use *The Party's Over* as a representative example of peak oil literature and see. I reread the book (for the first time in several years) as preparation for writing this essay, and the following are a few critical notes.

Chapters 1 and 2, which tell the tale of energy's role in ecology, history, and the economy, are the book's foundation. Leaving aside the question of how skillfully it's presented, it still impresses me as a story that deserves to be known and understood by everybody. There's very little that needs revision here.

Chapter 3, which explains peak oil, is pivotal to the book's overall argument. By current standards, much of this material is simplistic and dated. I fixed some problems in the revised 2005 edition, but that version itself is now stale. *The Party's Over* doesn't offer an original analysis of oil reserves or production data; instead it surveys the forecasts of "peakists" who were active at the time, many of whom are now less active or deceased.

The most obvious criticism that could be leveled at the book today is the simple observation that, as of 2014, world oil production is increasing, not declining. However, the following passage from page 118 of the 2003 edition points to just how accurate the leading peakists were in forecasting trends: "Colin Campbell estimates that extraction of conventional oil will peak before 2010; however, because more unconventional oil—including oil sands, heavy oil, and oil shale—will be produced during the coming decade, the total production of fossil-fuel liquids (conventional plus unconventional) will peak several years later. According to Jean Laherrère, that may happen as late as 2015." On page 121 of the book I explicitly endorsed the forecast of a peak sometime in the period between 2006 and 2015.

From today's perspective that's still an entirely defensible assessment of global oil supply prospects. Worldwide production of regular, conventional oil (excluding deepwater oil, tar sands, tight oil,
biofuels, and natural gas liquids such as propane) did indeed begin a
gentle, continuing decline around 2006, and a peak for all petroleum
liquids by 2015 is still likely though by no means certain. True, no
peak oil theorist in 2003 was forecasting that US petroleum production would take off in 2011 due to the hydraulic fracturing and
horizontal drilling of tight (low-permeability) oil-bearing rock formations in North Dakota and Texas. But tight oil (and tar sands,
and deepwater oil) are substantially different from the conventional
resources that drillers targeted in previous decades: they offer a low
energy return on the energy invested in production (EROEI), require high rates of up-front investment, and imply increased environmental costs and risks. Tight-oil wells show such steep production
decline rates that a peak followed by a sharp drop in output from the
Bakken and Eagle Ford plays—which have driven the recent boom in
US production—is probable in just the next few years.[8] Meanwhile,
the ongoing erosion of global extraction rates of regular, conventional crude means that an ever-larger proportion of total supplies
must come from unconventional sources. Conventional oil, with its
high EROEI and low production cost, fueled unprecedented levels
of economic growth during the twentieth century. That party is indeed over.

On page 117, I summarized Colin Campbell's view that "the next
decade will be a 'plateau' period, in which recurring economic reces-
sions will result in lowered energy demand, which will in turn temporarily mask the underlying depletion trend." That forecast appears to
have been spot on. Meanwhile, Daniel Yergin (of energy consultants
IHS CERA) and other petroleum industry-friendly energy commentators now tell us that peak oil is nothing to worry about because,
instead of a peaking of crude *supply*, we are instead seeing *peak demand*, as consumption of oil in the United States, Europe, and Japan
has fallen.[9] Why? Yergin and company cite improvements in vehicle

fuel efficiency, but in reality most of the reduction in oil consumption in the older industrial countries has come about simply because fuel prices are so high that people are driving less: they can't afford to fill the tank as often.[10] And prices are high because the only new sources of oil available to the industry are ones that are very expensive to develop. Analysts critical of peak oil failed to predict that petroleum prices would skyrocket to such an extent; indeed, during the past decade Daniel Yergin himself repeatedly (and wrongly) forecast falling oil prices.[11] "Peak oil demand" appears merely to be a rhetorical device that admits the reality of peak oil implicitly while denying it explicitly (we will return to this subject in "The Purposely Confusing World of Energy Politics" later in this book).

Meanwhile a comparison of forecasts by the peakists and their critics shows the former were generally far more successful in modeling oil production and price trends.[12]

The critics say peakists (like me) neglect basic economics: as oil prices go up, more supply comes on the market. This is correct up to a point; again, no peak oiler I know specifically foresaw the scale of the current US tight oil boom. However, Campbell and Laherrère did clearly forecast that higher prices would promote the development of unconventional petroleum sources (that's why Laherrère pegged the peak of "all liquids" several years later than the peak for regular crude). On the other hand, the peak oil critics themselves showed a lack of understanding of economic reality by ignoring the feedback between oil prices and the economy as a whole. Energy is what moves the economy; money is just a means of keeping track of wealth. Economics 101 tells us that supply of and demand for a commodity like oil (which happens to be our primary energy source) must converge at the current market price, but no economist can guarantee that the price will be affordable to society. High oil prices are sand in the gears of the economy.[13] As the oil industry is forced to spend ever more money to access ever-lower-quality resources, the result is a general trend toward economic stagnation. None of the peak oil deniers warned us about this.

The petroleum industry has undergone a profound shift in the past decade. Levels of investment in exploration and production have doubled, as have rates of drilling, but output has risen only modestly—and all of the increase has come from costly, problematic, unconventional sources. The world's ten largest publicly traded oil companies have collectively seen their production decline by more than 25 percent since 2004.[14] And the industry has taken on far more debt: this is especially true for the smaller companies that specialize in producing tight oil. The peak oil critics did not foresee this industry transformation at all, but anyone who read "The End of Cheap Oil" carefully in 1998, or *The Party's Over* in 2003, should have done so.

So much for Chapter 3. The following chapter discusses non-petroleum sources of energy, highlighting their various drawbacks and strengths. The section on natural gas requires substantial revision in light of the recent boom in US shale gas production (which I examine in my latest book, *Snake Oil: How Fracking's False Promise of Plenty Imperils Our Future*); otherwise, aside from the need for a general updating, there's little cause here for author embarrassment ten years on.

Chapter 5, "A Banquet of Consequences," discusses the likely societal impact of peak oil. While some of the more alarmist peak oil authors who were blogging during the years 2005 to 2010 suggested (or seemed to suggest) that society would effectively collapse before decade's end, *The Party's Over* paints a picture of developments likely to transpire over a longer period, from now until about 2050. A decline in available, cheap oil will impact the financial economy, agriculture, and transportation. We've already seen some problems along these lines as a result of oil prices exceeding a hundred dollars a barrel; more are on the way. There's not a lot here that needs revision ten years after the book's publication.

The final chapter, "Managing the Collapse," offers suggestions for what individuals, communities, and society as a whole might do to answer the challenge of peak oil and adapt to having less energy overall. If I were writing or rewriting this material today, I would point to recent efforts to prepare for the peak such as those organized by the

Transition Initiatives or by the city-sponsored Peak Oil Task Forces of Portland, Oakland, San Francisco, and Bloomington, Indiana. And I would cite several more recent books that do part or all of what this chapter attempted, but succeed more fully, elegantly, and entertainingly—such as Rob Hopkins's *Transition Handbook* and Albert Bates's *Post-Petroleum Survival Guide and Cookbook*.

One possible criticism of the book: while it briefly discusses climate change, it does so at insufficient length. This issue now dominates just about all energy policy discussions and deserved a more thorough treatment.

Altogether, nevertheless, *The Party's Over* fares pretty decently upon today's rereading—even if I do say so myself!

Reflection: Lessons from the Peak Oil Decade

What has been achieved in ten years by efforts to warn the world about peak oil? The book authors and bloggers who turned the subject of oil depletion into a cottage industry inspired hundreds of thousands—perhaps millions—of individuals worldwide to change their thinking, patterns of consumption, and expectations about the future. Some who read about peak oil changed careers or fields of study at university.

We peakists also changed the energy conversation: *peak oil* has become a recognized term and concept. In a way, the current "Peak Oil Is Dead" campaign is a testament to our success: the petroleum industry's public relations arm has been forced to expend resources putting out a fire that hardly amounted to a spark a decade ago. As a result of that campaign, even more people have heard of peak oil than before— though most probably have a highly erroneous impression of it.

Peak oil bashing is not entirely the province of the petroleum industry: a very few leftist writers have argued that peakism is a conspiracy covertly organized by the industry itself to talk up prices (and profits) through invoking a false anticipation of scarcity.[15] In my years researching the topic and my many interactions with oil geologists, engineers, and company representatives, I have seen no evidence to support this view. Instead I've heard industry spokespeople use every possible rhetorical trick to draw attention away from the process and consequences of oil depletion.

Peakists within the industry are usually technical staff (usually geologists, seldom economists, and never PR professionals) and are only free to speak out on the subject once they've retired. The industry has two big reasons to hate peak oil. First, company stock prices are tied to the value of booked oil reserves; if the public (and government regulators) were to become convinced that those reserves were problematic, the companies' ability to raise money would be seriously compromised—and oil companies need to raise lots of money these days to find and produce ever-lower-quality resources. It's thus in the interest of companies to maintain an impression of (at least potential) abundance. Second, the industry doesn't want society to mount a serious effort to reduce its dependence on petroleum. People who take peak oil seriously are understandably nervous about petroleum dependency and are looking for a way out. The oil industry wants more highways, not more streetcars and bicycles; more pipelines, not more solar panels.

Resistance to the idea of peak oil has also come from mainstream economists. That's because (as *The Party's Over* explained on pages 169–72) peak oil effectively means the end of economic growth as we knew it during the 20th century. Growth is sacred to most economists: even credentialed insiders (economists like Jeff Rubin or investment fund managers like Jeremy Grantham) who question growth get pilloried by the priesthood. Politicians and business leaders love growth and hate anything that might call into question our ability to maintain it from here to eternity. For this reason alone, peak oil theory was destined for a public thrashing regardless of its accuracy.

Some within the peakist movement now say the term *peak oil* has outlived its usefulness, and it is time to find new ways to name and frame the issues of resource depletion and energy scarcity. Others say we've invested years of effort in popularizing the term and we're irrevocably identified with it anyway, so we simply have to do what we can to rehabilitate it. Either way, many peakists are pretty dispirited these days.

Our public relations failure pales in comparison to our inability to achieve our real goal—which was to convince society to prepare for the end of the brief age of cheap, abundant energy. While individuals, a few organizations, and a handful of communities have indeed responded, the numbers are relatively small. National governments have done almost nothing. The best broad-scale policy would have been an international agreement to reduce production and consumption of oil in tandem (this idea was mooted as a proposal known as the Uppsala Protocol, the Rimini Protocol, or The Oil Depletion Protocol[16]). But aside from resolutions of support from the Portuguese parliament and the city councils of Portland, Oakland, and San Francisco, there has been no real governmental interest in such an agreement.

What have I learned? That it's hard to change the direction of society, but—given what's at stake—that it's worth trying. Knowing what I knew in 2003, I could not have lived with myself during the past dozen years had I not at least attempted to alert the general populace and tried to change the thinking of policy makers.

It's impossible to foresee how far the ripples created by the efforts undertaken to raise awareness about our precarious energy ecology will spread. Even though society is still headed toward a wrenching collision with resource limits, educated and aware people have begun to build low-energy alternative food, transport, and building systems that can support organized human life during the transition to a post-fossil-fuel future. How much more can be done in the time we still have? Let's find out.

For a book, it's the end of a decade. But it's not the end of the story.

— SEPTEMBER 2013

2

▶ THE GROSS SOCIETY

SEEING ONLY ITS TITLE, A PROSPECTIVE READER MIGHT GUESS this essay is about our nation's epidemic of obesity. Or could it be a sarcastic observation on the evolution of Lyndon Johnson's *Great Society*? Might it be a jeremiad about the *gross* (i.e., offensive and disgusting) ways we waste and overconsume natural resources, or a comment on current television trends? There's plenty to be said on all those scores.

No, the definition of *gross* I have in mind is "exclusive of deductions," as in *gross profits* versus *net profits*. The profits we'll be considering come in the forms not just of money but, more crucially, of energy. Sound boring? Well, you may be surprised.

Here's my thesis: As a society, we are entering the early stages of energy impoverishment. It's hard to overstate just how serious a threat this is to every aspect of our current way of life. But the problem is hidden from view by *gross* oil and natural gas production numbers that look and feel just fine—good enough to crow about.

President Obama did plenty of crowing in his 2014 State of the Union address, where he touted "More oil produced at home than we buy from the rest of the world—the first time that's happened in nearly twenty years." It's true: US crude oil production increased from about 5 million barrels per day (mb/d) to nearly 7.75 mb/d from 2009 through 2013 (with imports still over 7.5 mb/d). And American natural gas production has been at an all-time high. Energy problem? What energy problem?

While these gross numbers appear splendid, when you look at *net* numbers things go pear-shaped, as the British say.

Our economy is 100 percent dependent on energy: with more and cheaper energy, the economy booms; with less and costlier energy, it wilts. When the electricity grid goes down or the gasoline pumps run dry, the economy simply stops in its tracks.

But the situation is actually a bit more complicated, because *it takes energy to get energy*. It takes diesel fuel to drill oil wells; it takes electricity to build solar panels. The energy that's left over—once we've fueled production of energy—makes possible all the things people want and need to do. It's *net* energy, not *gross* energy, that does society's work.

Before the advent of fossil fuels, agriculture was our main energy source, and the average net gain from the work of energy production was minimal. Farmers grew food for people—who did a lot of manual work in those days—and also for horses and oxen, whose muscles provided motive power for farm machinery and for land transport via carts and carriages. Because margins were small, most people had to toil in the fields in order to produce enough surplus to enable a small minority of folks to live in towns and specialize in arts and crafts (including statecraft and soldiery).

In contrast, the early years of the fossil fuel era saw astounding energy profits. Wildcat oil drillers could invest a few thousand dollars in equipment and drilling leases and, if they struck black gold, become millionaires almost overnight. If you want a taste of what that was like, watch the classic 1940 film *Boom Town*, with Clark Gable and Claudette Colbert.[1]

Huge energy returns on both energy and financial investments in drilling made the fossil fuel revolution the biggest event in economic history. Suddenly society was awash with surplus energy.

Cheap energy plus a little invention yielded mechanization. Farming became an increasingly mechanized (i.e., fossil-fueled) occupation, which meant fewer field laborers were needed. People left farms and moved to cities, where they got jobs on powered assembly lines manufacturing an explosively expanding array of consumer goods, including labor-saving (i.e., energy-consuming) home machinery like electric vacuum cleaners and clothes washers. Household machines helped free women to participate in the work force. The middle class mushroomed. Little Henry and Henrietta, whose grandparents had spent their lives plowing, harvesting, cooking, and cleaning, could now contemplate careers as biologists, sculptors, heart specialists, bankers, concert violinists, professors of medieval French literature—whatever! Human ambition and aspiration appeared to know no bounds.

Unfortunately, there are a couple of problems with fossil fuels. The first is that they cause climate change and thereby cast a pall over

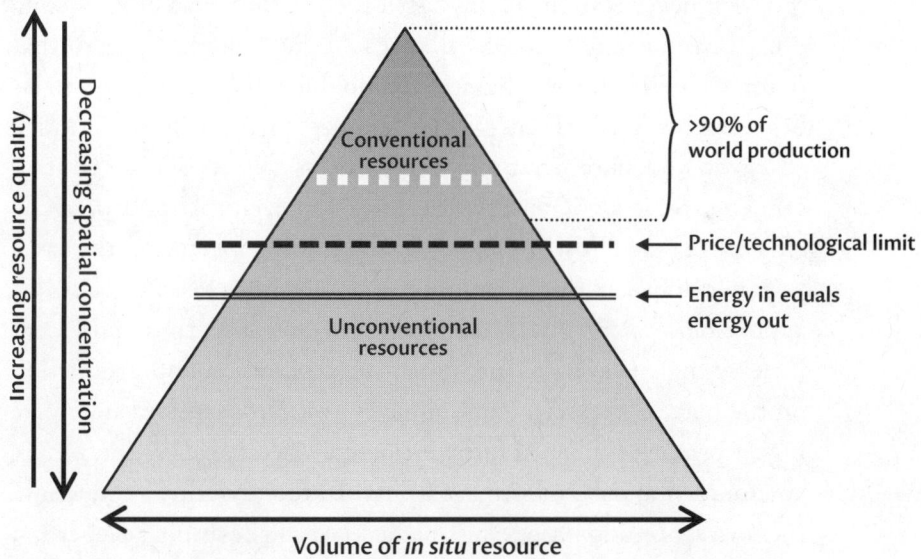

FIGURE 1: The pyramid of oil and gas resource volume versus resource quality. This graphic illustrates the relationship of *in situ* resource volumes to the distribution of conventional and unconventional accumulations, and the generally declining net energy and increasing difficulty of extraction as volumes increase lower in the pyramid. Source: J. David Hughes, *Drill, Baby, Drill: Can Unconventional Fuels Usher in a New Era of Energy Abundance?*, Post Carbon Institute, 2013.

the prospects of civilized human existence on planet Earth—but let's set that irritating thought aside for a moment. The other problem is that these fuels are finite in quantity and of variable quality; we have extracted them using the *low-hanging fruit* principle, going after the highest quality, cheapest-to-produce oil, coal, and natural gas first, and leaving the lower quality, more expensive, and harder-to-extract fuels for later. Now, it's *later*.

It's helpful to visualize this best-first principle by way of a diagram of what geologists call the *resource pyramid*. Extractive industries typically start at the top of the pyramid and work their way down. This was the case at the beginning of the Industrial Revolution, when coal miners exploited only the very best coal seams, and it's also true today as drillers in the Bakken oil play in North Dakota concentrate their efforts in core areas within that play where per-well production rates are highest.

We'll never run out of any fossil fuel, in the sense of extracting every last molecule of coal, oil, or gas. Long before we get to that point, we will confront the dreaded double line in the diagram, labeled "energy in equals energy out." At that stage, it will cost as much energy to find, pump, transport, and process a barrel of oil as the oil's refined products will yield when burned in even the most perfectly efficient engine (I use oil merely as the most apt example; the same principle applies for coal, natural gas, or any other fossil fuel). As we approach the energy break-even point, we can expect the requirement for ever-higher levels of investment in exploration and production on the part of the petroleum industry; we can therefore anticipate higher prices for finished fuels. Incidentally, we can also expect more environmental risk and damage from the process of fuel "production" (i.e., extraction and processing), because we will be drilling deeper and going to the ends of the Earth to find the last remaining deposits, and we will be burning ever-dirtier fuels.

Right now that's exactly what *is* happening.

While America's current gross oil production numbers appear rosy, from an energy accounting perspective the figures are frightening: energy profit margins are declining fast.

Each year, a greater percentage of US oil production comes from unconventional sources—primarily tight oil and deepwater oil.[2] Compared to conventional oil from most onshore, vertical wells, these sources demand much higher capital investment per barrel produced. Tight oil wells typically require directional drilling and hydraulic fracturing ("fracking"), which take lots of money and energy (not to mention water); initial production rates per well are modest, and production from each well tends to decline quickly. Therefore more wells have to be drilled continually in order to maintain a constant rate of flow. This has been called the "Red Queen" syndrome, after a passage in Lewis Carroll's *Through the Looking-Glass*. In the story, the fictional Red Queen runs at top speed but never gets anywhere; she explains to Alice, "It takes all the running you can do, to keep in the same place." Similarly, it will soon take all the drilling the industry can do just to keep production in the fracking fields steady. But the plateau won't last long; as the best drilling areas become saturated with wells and companies are forced toward the peripheries of fuel-bearing geological formations, costs will rise and production will fall. When, exactly, will the decline begin? Probably before the end of this decade.[3]

Deepwater production is expensive too: it involves operating in miles of ocean water on giant drilling and production rigs.[4] It is also both environmentally and financially risky, as BP discovered in 2010 in the Gulf of Mexico.

Canada's tar sands require special energy-intensive processing in order to yield usable fuels. Unless oil prices remain at current stratospheric levels, significant expansion of tar sands operations may be uneconomic.

America is turning increasingly to unconventional oil because conventional sources of petroleum are drying up. The United States is where the oil business started and, in the past century-and-a-half, more oil wells have been drilled here than in the rest of the world's countries put together. In terms of our resource pyramid diagram, the United States has drilled through the top "conventional resources" triangle and down to the thick dashed line labeled "price/technological limit." At this point, significantly new technology is required to extract more oil (of which there is plenty—just look how much of the total pyramid is left!), and this comes at a higher financial cost, not just to the industry but ultimately to society as a whole.[5] Yet society cannot afford oil that's arbitrarily expensive: the "price/technological limit" can be moved up to a point, but we may be reaching the frontiers of affordability.

Lower energy profits from unconventional oil inevitably show up in the financials of oil companies. Between 1998 and 2005, the industry invested $1.5 trillion in exploration and production, and this investment yielded 8.6 million barrels per day in additional world oil production. Between 2005 and 2013, the industry spent $4 trillion on E&P, yet this more-than-doubled investment produced only 4 mb/d in added production.[6]

It gets worse: all net new production during the 2005–13 period was from unconventional sources (primarily tight oil from the United States and tar sands from Canada); of the $4 trillion spent since 2005, it took $350 billion to achieve a bump in their production. Subtracting unconventionals from the total, world oil production actually fell by about a million barrels a day during these years. That means the oil industry spent more than $3.5 trillion to achieve a *decline* in overall conventional production.

The year 2013 was one of the worst ever for new discoveries, and companies are cutting exploration budgets (if there's nothing worth finding, why waste money?). A recent Reuters article quoted Tim Dodson, the exploration chief of Statoil, the world's top conventional explorer: "It is becoming increasingly difficult to find new oil and gas, and in particular new oil.... The discoveries tend to be somewhat smaller, more complex, more remote, so it is very difficult to see a reversal of that trend.... The industry at large will probably struggle going forward with reserve replacement."[7]

Here is how energy analyst Mark Lewis and US Army lieutenant colonel Daniel L. Davis described the situation in a recent article in the *Financial Times*:

> The 2013 [*World Energy Outlook*, published by the International Energy Agency] has the oil industry's upstream [capital expenditure] rising by nearly 180 per cent since 2000, but the global oil supply (adjusted for energy content) by only 14 per cent. The most straightforward interpretation of this data is that the economics of oil have become completely dislocated from historic norms since 2000 (and especially since 2005), with the industry investing at exponentially higher rates for increasingly small incremental yields of energy.[8]

The squeeze is also being felt by the global economy, which has sputtered ever since oil prices began their steep march up to the "new normal" of $90–$110 per barrel (more about this below).

The costs of oil exploration and production are currently rising at about 10.9 percent per year, according to Steve Kopits of the energy analytics firm Douglas-Westwood.[9] This is squeezing the industry's profit margins, since it's getting ever harder to pass these costs on to consumers.

In 2010, *The Economist* magazine discussed rising costs of energy production, musing that "the direction of change seems clear. If the world were a giant company, its return on capital would be falling."[10]

Tim Morgan, formerly of the London-based brokerage Tullett Prebon (whose customers consist primarily of investment banks), explored the averaged energy return on energy investment (EROEI) of global energy sources in one of his company's *Strategy Insights* reports (regrettably failing to cite the work of Charles Hall, on which he was basing his calculations), noting in 2013:

> For 2020, our projected EROEI (of 11.5:1) [would] mean that the share of GDP absorbed by energy costs would have

escalated to about 9.6 percent from around 6.7 percent today. Our projections further suggest that energy costs could absorb almost 15 percent of GDP (at an EROEI of 7.7:1) by 2030.... [T]he critical relationship between energy production and the energy cost of extraction is now deteriorating so rapidly that the economy as we have known it for more than two centuries is beginning to unravel.[11]

From an energy accounting perspective, the situation is in one respect actually worst in North America—which is deeply ironic since it's here that production has grown most in the past five years, and here that the industry is most boastful of its achievements. Yet the average energy profit ratio for US oil production has fallen from 100:1 to 10:1,[12] and the downward trend is accelerating as more and more oil comes from tight deposits (shale) and deepwater. Canada's prospects are perhaps even more dismal than those of the United States: the tar sands of Alberta have an EROEI that ranges from 3.2:1 to 5:1.[13]

A five-to-one profit ratio might be spectacular in the financial world, but in energy terms this is alarming. Everything we do in industrial societies—education, health care, research, manufacturing, transportation—uses energy. Unless our *investment of energy in producing more energy* yields an averaged profit ratio of roughly 10:1 or more, it may not be possible to maintain an industrial (as opposed to an agrarian) mode of societal organization over the long run.[14]

None of the unconventional sources that the petroleum industry is turning toward (tight oil, tar sands, deepwater) would have been developed absent the context of high oil prices, which deliver more revenue to oil companies; it's those revenues that fund ever-bigger investments in technology. But older industrial economies like the United States and the European Union tend to stall out if oil costs too much, and that reduces energy demand; this "demand destruction" safety valve has (so far) set a limit on global petroleum prices. Yet for the major oil companies, prices are currently not high enough to pay for the development of new projects in the Arctic or in ultra-deepwater; this is another reason the majors are cutting back on exploration investments.[15]

For everyone else, though, oil prices are plenty high. Soaring fuel prices wallop airlines, the tourism industry, and farmers. Even real estate prices can be impacted: as gasoline gets more expensive, the lure of distant suburbs for prospective homebuyers wanes. It's more than mere coincidence that the US housing bubble burst in 2008, just as oil prices hit their all-time high.

Rising gasoline prices (since 2005) have led to a reduction in the average number of miles traveled by US vehicles annually,[16] a trend toward less driving by young people,[17] and efforts on the part of the auto industry to produce more fuel-efficient vehicles.[18] Altogether, American oil consumption is today roughly 20 percent below what it would have been if growth trends in the previous decades had continued.[19]

To people concerned about climate change, much of this sounds like good news. Oil companies' spending is up but profits are down. Gasoline is more expensive and consumption has declined. Hooray!

There's just one catch. None of this is happening as a result of long-range, comprehensive planning. And it will take a lot of planning and effort to minimize the human impact of a societal shift from relative energy abundance to relative energy scarcity. In fact, there is virtually no discussion occurring among officials about the larger economic implications of declining energy returns on investment. Indeed, rather than soberly assessing the situation and its imminent economic challenges, our policy makers are stuck in a state of public relations-induced euphoria, high on temporarily spiking *gross* US oil and gas production numbers.

The obvious solution to declining fossil fuel returns on investment is to transition to alternative energy sources as quickly as possible. We'll have to do this anyway to address the climate crisis. But from an energy accounting point of view, it may not offer much help.

Renewable energy sources like solar and wind have characteristics very different from those of fossil fuels: the former are intermittent, while the latter are available on demand.[20] Solar and wind can't affordably power airliners or eighteen-wheel trucks. Moreover, many renewable energy sources have a relatively low energy profit ratio.

One of the indicators of low or declining energy returns on energy investment is a greater requirement for human labor in the energy production process. In an economy suffering from high unemployment, this may seem like a boon. Indeed, wind and solar energy are often touted as job creators,[21] employing more people than the coal and oil industries put together (even though they produce far less energy for society). Yes, jobs are good. But what would happen if we went all the way back to the average energy returns-on-investment of agrarian times? There'd certainly be plenty of work needing to be done. But we would be living in a society very different from the one we're accustomed to, one in which most people are full-time energy producers and society is able to support relatively few specialists in other activities. Granted, that's probably an exaggeration of our real prospects: at least some renewable energy sources can give us higher returns than were common in the agrarian era. However, they won't power a rerun of *Dallas*. This will be a simpler, slower, and poorer economy.

If our economy runs on energy, and our energy prospects are gloomy, how is it that the economy is *recovering*?

The simplest answer is, *it's not*—except as measured by a few misleading gross statistics. Each month the Bureau of Labor Statistics releases figures for new jobs created, and the numbers look relatively good at first glance (288,000 net new jobs for April 2014, for example[22]). But most of these new jobs pay less than jobs that were lost in recent years. And unemployment statistics don't include people who've given up looking for work. Labor force participation rates are at the lowest level in 35 years.[23]

All told, according to a recent Gallup poll, a majority of Americans say they are worse off today than they were a year ago (a minority say their situation has improved).[24]

Claims of economic recovery fixate primarily on one number: gross domestic product, or GDP. That number is going up, albeit at an anemic pace in comparison with rates common in the 20th century; hence, the economy is said to be growing. But what does this really mean? When GDP rises, that indicates more money is flowing through the economy. Typically, a higher GDP equates to more consumption of goods and services, and therefore more jobs. What's not to like about that?

A couple of things. First, there are ways of making GDP grow that don't actually improve people's lives. Economist Herman Daly calls this "uneconomic growth." For example, if we spend money on rebuilding after a natural disaster, or on prisons or armaments or cancer treatment, GDP rises. But who wants more natural disasters, crime, wars, or cancer? Historically, the burning of ever more fossil fuels was closely tied to GDP expansion, but now we face the prospect of devastating climate change if we continue increasing our burn rate. To the extent GDP growth is based on fossil fuel consumption, when GDP goes up we're actually worse off because of it. Altogether, *gross domestic product* does a really bad job of capturing how our economy is doing on a *net* basis. In fact, Daly figures that just about all our current GDP growth is uneconomic.[25]

Second, a growing money supply (which is implied by GDP growth) depends upon the expansion of credit. Another way to say this is: a rising GDP (in any country with a floating exchange rate) entails increasing levels of outstanding debt. Historical statistics bear this out.[26] But is any society able to expand its debt endlessly?

If there were indeed limits to a country's ability to perpetually grow GDP by increasing its total debt (government plus private), a warning sign would likely come in the form of a trend toward diminishing GDP returns on each new unit of credit created. Bingo: that's exactly what we've been seeing in the United States in recent years. Back in the 1960s, each dollar of increase in total US debt was reflected in nearly a dollar of rise in GDP. By 2000, each new dollar of debt corresponded with only 20 cents of GDP growth. The trend line looked set to reach zero by about 2015.[27]

Meanwhile, it seems that Americans have taken on about as much household debt as they can manage, as rates of consumer borrowing have been stuck in neutral since the start of the Great Recession. To keep debt growing (and the economy expanding, if only statistically), the Federal Reserve has kept interest rates low by creating up to $85 billion per month through a mere adjustment of its ledgers (yes, it can do that); it uses the money to buy Treasury bills (US government debt) from Wall Street banks. When interest rates are low, people find it easier to buy houses and cars (hence the recent rise in house prices and the auto industry's rebound); it also makes it cheaper for the government to borrow—and, in case you haven't noticed, the federal government has borrowed a lot lately. The Fed's quantitative easing (QE) program (by which that entity simply creates tens of billions of dollars a month with a few computer keystrokes, using much of the money to buy government debt instruments) props up the banks, the auto companies, the housing market, and the Treasury. But with overall consumer spending still anemic, the trillions of dollars the Fed has created cumulatively have generally not been loaned out to households and small businesses; instead, they've simply pooled up in the big banks. This is money that's constantly prowling for significant financial returns, nearly all of which go to the "one percenters."[28] Fed policy has thus generated a stock market bubble, as well as a bubble of investments in emerging markets, and these can only continue to inflate for as long as QE persists.[29]

The only way to keep these bubbles from growing and eventually bursting (with attendant financial toxicity spilling over into the rest of the economy) is to stop QE. But doing that will undermine the "recovery," such as it is, and might even send the economy careening into depression. The Fed's solution to this "damned if you do, damned if you don't" quandary is to "taper" QE, reducing it gradually over time.

However, this doesn't really solve anything; it's just a way to delay and pretend.

With money as with energy, we're doing extremely well at keeping up appearances by characterizing our situation with a few cherry-picked numbers. But behind the jolly statistics lurks a menacing reality. Collectively, we're like a dietician who has adopted the attitude: *the more you weigh, the healthier you are!* How gross would that be?

The world is changing. Cheap, high-EROEI energy and genuine economic growth are disappearing. Rather than recognizing this fact, we hide it from ourselves with misleading figures. All that this does is make it harder to adapt to our new reality.

The irony is, if we recognized the trends and did a little planning, there could be an upside to all of this. We've become overspecialized anyway. We teach our kids to operate machines so sophisticated that almost no one can build one from scratch, but not how to cook, sew, repair broken tools, or grow food. We seem to be less happy year by year.[30] We're overcrowded, and continuing population growth only makes matters worse.[31] Why not encourage family planning instead? Studies suggest we could dial back on consumption and be more satisfied with our lives.[32]

What would the world look and feel like if we deliberately and intelligently nudged the brakes on material consumption, reduced our energy throughput, and relearned some general skills? Quite a few people have already done the relevant experiment. Take an online virtual tour of Dancing Rabbit ecovillage in northeast Missouri,[33] or Lakabe in northern Spain.[34] But you don't have to move to an ecovillage to join in the fun; there are thousands of Transition Initiatives worldwide running essentially the same experiment in ordinary towns and cities, just not so intensively.[35] Take a look at the website resilience.org any day of the week to see reports on these experiments, and tips on what you could do to adapt more successfully to our new economic reality.

All of these efforts have a couple of things in common: First, they entail a lot of hard work and (according to what I hear) yield considerable satisfaction. Second, they are self-organized and self-directed, not funded or overseen by government.

The latter point is crucial—not because government is inherently wicked, but because it's just not likely to be of much help in present circumstances. That's because our political system is currently too broken to grasp the nature of the problems facing us.[36] Which is unfortunate, because even a little large-scale planning and support could help; without it, we can be sure the transition will be more chaotic than necessary, and a lot of people will be hurt needlessly.

Quite simply, we must learn to be successfully and happily poorer. For people in wealthy industrialized countries, this will require a major adjustment in thinking. When it comes to energy, we have deluded ourselves into believing that gross is the same as net. That's because in the early days of fossil fuels, it very nearly was. But now we have to go back to thinking the way people did when energy profit margins were smaller. We must learn to operate within budgets and limits.

This means decentralization, simplification, and localization. Becoming less reliant on debt, paying as we go. It means living closer to the ground, learning general skills, and keeping a hand in basic productive activities like growing food.

Think of our future as the Lean Society.

We can make this transition successfully, if not happily, if enough of us embrace Lean Society thinking and habits. But things likely won't go well at all if we continue to hide reality from ourselves with gross numbers that delay our adaptation to accelerating, inevitable trends.

— APRIL 2014

3

▶ VISUALIZE GASOLINE

NEXT TIME YOU FIND YOURSELF IN TRAFFIC, TRY THIS NIFTY thought exercise. Ignore the cars within your field of vision and imagine instead the contents of their fuel tanks. Visualize gasoline flowing up and down the highway.

Let's assume the typical American car carries seven gallons of refined petroleum product in its tank at any given moment (a fifteen-gallon tank half-full). That's a lot of liquid to be carting around. In fact, gasoline is the second-most-consumed fluid in the United States, after water. Each American household consumes an average of 350 gallons of water per day and 2.5 gallons of gasoline; milk, coffee, and beer clock in at 0.15 gallons, 0.12 gallons, and 0.1 gallons, respectively.

If you do this visualization exercise, you might find yourself seeing rivulets, streams, and—in the case of big freeways—*rivers* of gasoline coursing across the land. For the United States as a whole, four hundred million gallons of gasoline enter and leave the flow every day. But, since we routinely carry more gasoline with us than we intend to use immediately, the total amount in car gas tanks at any given moment is roughly seven times larger, so that America's gasoline rivers slosh with 2.8 billion gallons on any given day.

A real river or stream is the spine of a watershed and the heart of a riparian ecosystem. Trees, shrubs, insects and their larvae, fish, birds, amphibians, and mammals all derive their livelihoods from flowing water.

A river of gasoline is sterile by comparison, even though petroleum itself is primarily composed of the same two elements as living things: carbon and hydrogen. Oil is a *fossil* fuel, after all, made of heaps and heaps of dead plankton and algae compressed and heated over millions of years so that carbohydrates became hydrocarbons. Gasoline rivers are no place for nonhuman life forms: only the most daring of weeds and foolhardy of animals venture there, with the latter often ending up as road kill. Indeed, highways could be thought of as rivers of death.

Water makes itself seen and felt as it falls from the sky and collects in puddles, ponds, lakes, and oceans. The tiny fraction of Earth's water that enters municipal delivery systems temporarily disappears into a maze of pipes but soon reemerges at the ends of faucets and showerheads.

Gasoline is covert and furtive by comparison. Oil emerges from wells and, via pipelines, enters refineries; from these, gasoline gushes through more pipes that carry it to regional distribution centers, whence it is delivered by tanker truck to filling stations. We travel to those stations to dispense gas by hose into the tanks of our cars; from those tanks it is delivered to its final moment of combustion within the engine. At no point along its path is oil or gasoline customarily exposed to public view.

What we see instead, for the most part, is the automobile—a painstakingly crafted exoskeleton that carries gasoline and humans from place to place—and a landscape substantially altered to suit its demands. We obsess over our cars: they are our symbols of freedom and status. We judge them by the elegance of their design, their top speed, their acceleration. We revere their brand names: Mercedes, Ferrari, Jaguar, Bentley, Cadillac, Lexus. We take for granted the gasoline that makes them go, until a gauge or warning light on the dashboard forces us to pull over and buy more. Yet without gas there would be no point to the automobile; even the brawniest Porsche could do no more than ornament a driveway.

We complain about the price of gasoline, yet at four dollars per gallon it is cheaper than coffee, beer, or milk—cheaper even than most bottled water.

Unlike those other liquids, gasoline is explosive. It literally gives us a bang—and a fairly *big* bang, at that. Visualize slowly pushing your car miles at a time, your leg and arm muscles straining to move a ton or two of metal, and you may gain some appreciation for how much power is being released by each drop of the gasoline that normally speeds it down the road, with virtually no effort required on your part.

Visualize gasoline-powered civilization arising as if by some maniacally accelerated evolutionary process. It all began so recently, in the mid-19th century, and spread across the globe in mere decades. Automobiles mutated and competed for dominance on vast networks of roads built to accommodate them. Shopping malls and parking garages sprang up to attract and hold them. And powering it all was an ever-widening but mostly invisible river of gasoline—the poisonous blood of seven hundred million dinosaur-like machines that now dot landscapes around the world.

Visualize gasoline's combustion by-products spewing out of millions of tailpipes and into the air our children breathe. As we pump oil out of the ground we transfer ancient carbon from the Earth's crust into the atmosphere at a rate of 5.2 metric tons per car per year. A car that gets 25 miles per gallon of gasoline spews out 47 gallons of carbon dioxide for every mile it travels (at standard temperature and pressure). Like gasoline, carbon dioxide is invisible most of the time; you have to use your powers of visualization to see the thickening blanket of CO_2 that traps more and more of Earth's heat.

Visualize ancient subterranean oil reservoirs rapidly depleting, with half of Earth's entire inheritance of conventional crude converted to CO_2 and water during the lifetime of an average baby boomer (1950–2025). Already, nations are straining to adjust to declining oil abundance, searching for alternatives, and fighting over what's left. No, we're not *running out* of oil. We've only begun tapping tar sands, tight oil, and polar oil. But what's left, though impressive in quantity, will be expensive, risky, and slow to extract.

Visualize a time, years or decades from now, when machines designed to burn gasoline sit idle, rusting, abandoned. No, we *won't* quickly and easily switch to electric cars. For that to happen, the economy would have to keep growing, so that more and more people could afford to buy new (and more costly) automobiles. A more likely scenario: as fuel gets increasingly expensive the economy will falter, rendering the transition to electric cars too little, too late.

Visualize life without gasoline. You might as well start doing so now, at least in your imagination; soon enough, this will no longer be an exercise. Already prices are high and volatile. In coming years or decades we may see international conflicts that shut down big portions of the global oil trade for weeks or months at a time. Strategic reserves will be tapped. The government will commandeer supplies for the military and police. One way or another, you'll be using much less gasoline than you do today. How will your food be grown and transported? How will you get around? Will your job still exist? How will your community function?

Visualizing gasoline won't make more of it magically appear. But understanding the extent of our dependence on it helps us address our vulnerability to the inevitable process of depletion. Imagining a world without gasoline could be a useful first step in preparing for a future that's coming at us, whether we're ready or not.

— MAY 2012

▶ THE CLIMATE PR PUZZLE

I F WE HOPE TO AVERT A CLIMATE APOCALYPSE IN THE DECADES ahead, we must make fundamental changes to industrial society. Before these changes can be approved and implemented, citizens and policy makers must first come to understand that they are essential to our survival. Public relations (PR)—the management of the spread of information between an individual or organization and the public— will be an unavoidably necessary tool in this process.

But a PR message capable of persuading policy makers and citizens to end society's environmental rampage remains elusive. In this essay I hope to explore why an effective PR message is so hard to formulate, and how the whole project might be reconsidered.

Let's start with what needs to be conveyed. After years of research and thought, I would summarize our dilemma with three general conclusions:

Conclusion 1: Energy is the biggest single issue facing us as a species.[1] Global warming—by far the worst environmental challenge humans have ever confronted—results from our current fossil-fuel energy regime, and averting catastrophic climate change will require us to end our reliance on coal, oil, and natural gas. Ocean acidification is also a consequence of burning fossil fuels, and most other environmental crises (like nitrogen runoff pollution created by fertilizers made from fossil fuels, and most air pollution) can be traced to the same source. Therefore ending our addiction to fossil fuels is essential if we want future generations of humans (and countless other species) to inherit a habitable planet.

But these energy sources are also "unsustainable" in a more basic, economic sense of the term: oil, gas, and coal are depleting, nonrenewable resources. Already, depletion of the easy-and-cheap sources of petroleum that drove economic growth in the 20th century has led to persistently high oil prices, which are a drag on the economy. We have picked the low-hanging fruit of the world's petroleum resources, and as time goes on *all* sources of fossil energy will become more financially costly and environmentally risky to extract. This is a big problem because the economy is 100 percent dependent on energy. With lots of cheap energy, problems of all kinds are easy to solve (Running out of fresh water? Just build a desalination plant!); when energy becomes expensive and hard to get, problems multiply and converge.

One way or another, whether our concern is the environment or economic growth, it's mostly about energy.

Conclusion 2: We are headed toward a (nearly) all-renewable-energy economy one way or the other, and planning is essential if we want to get there in one piece.

If society is to avoid civilization-threatening levels of climate change, the use of fossil fuels will have to be reduced proactively by 80–90 percent by 2050.[2]

At the same time, despite the claims of abundance of unconventional fuels (shale gas, tight oil, tar sands) by the fossil fuel industry, evidence overwhelmingly shows that drillers are investing increasing effort to achieve diminishing returns.

Either way, fossil fuels are on their way out.

Most nations have concluded that nuclear power is too costly and risky, and supplies of uranium, the predominant fuel for nuclear power, are limited anyway. Thorium, breeder, fusion, and other nuclear alternatives may hold theoretical promise, but there is virtually no hope that we can resolve the remaining myriad practical challenges, commercialize the technologies, and deploy tens of thousands of new power plants within just a few decades.

That leaves renewable energy sources—solar, wind, hydro, geothermal, tidal, and wave power—to power the economy of the future.

Conclusion 3: In the process of transition, the ways that society *uses* energy must change at least as much as the ways society *produces* energy.

Every energy source possesses a unique set of characteristics: some sources are more portable than others, or more concentrated, intermittent, scalable, diffuse, renewable, environmentally risky, or expensive. We have built our current economy to take advantage of the special properties of fossil fuels. The renewable energy sources that are available to replace oil, gas, and coal have very different characteristics and will therefore tend to support a different kind of economy—one that is less mobile, more rooted in place; less globalized, more localized; less when-we-want-it, more when-it's-available; less engineered, more organic.

At the same time, the sheer *quantity* of energy that will be available during the transition from fossil to renewable sources is in doubt. While ever-more-rapid rates of extraction of fossil fuels powered a growing economy during the 20th century, society will struggle to maintain current levels of total energy production in the 21st, let alone grow them to meet projected demand. Indeed, there are credible scenarios in which available energy could decline significantly. And we will have to invest a lot of the fossil energy we *do* have in building post-fossil energy infrastructure. Energy efficiency can help along the way, but only marginally.

The global economy will almost certainly stagnate or contract accordingly.

There it is. It is a complicated message. I've just conveyed it in under seven hundred words punctuated by three short summary sentences. (And here's a summation of the summation: it's all about energy; renewables are the future; growth is over.) However, only readers with a lot of prior knowledge will be able to truly understand some of these words and phrases. And many people who are capable of making sense of what I've written would disagree with, or dismiss, much of it. The message faces a tough audience, and it flies against deep-seated interests.

Many economists and politicians don't buy the assertion that energy is at the core of our species-wide survival challenge. They think the game of human success-or-failure revolves around money, military power, or technological advancement. If we toggle prices, taxes, and interest rates; maintain proper trade rules; invest in technology research and development (R&D); and discourage military challenges to the current international order, then growth can continue indefinitely and everything will be fine. Climate change and resource depletion are peripheral problems that can be dealt with through pricing mechanisms or regulations.

Fossil fuel companies may understand the importance of energy, but they have a powerful incentive to avoid acceptance of the message that "renewables are the future." If humanity is headed toward an all-renewable energy economy, then their business has no future. The industry's strategy for diverting the general public's buy-in to Conclusion 2 is to claim that there is plenty of oil, gas, and coal available to fuel society for decades to come.

Some policy wonks buy "it's all about energy" but are jittery about "renewables are the future" and won't go anywhere near "growth is over." A few of these folks like to think of themselves as environmentalists (sometimes calling themselves "bright green")—including the Breakthrough Institute and writers like Stewart Brand and Mark Lynas. A majority of government officials are effectively in the same camp, viewing nuclear power, natural gas, carbon capture and storage ("clean coal"), and further technological innovation as pathways to solving the climate crisis without any need to curtail economic growth.

Other environment-friendly folks buy "it's all about energy" and "renewables are the future" but still remain allergic to the notion that "growth is over." They say we can transition to 100 percent renewable power with no sacrifice in terms of economic growth, comfort, or convenience. Stanford professor Mark Jacobson[3] and Amory Lovins of Rocky Mountain Institute are leaders of this chorus. Theirs is a reassuring message, but if it doesn't happen to be factually true (and there are many energy experts who argue persuasively that it isn't), then it's of limited helpfulness because it fails to recommend the kinds or degrees of change in energy usage that are essential to a successful transition.

The general public tends to listen to one or another of these groups, all of which agree that the climate and energy challenge of the 21st century can be met without sacrificing economic growth. This widespread aversion to the "growth is over" conclusion is entirely understandable: during the last century, the economies of industrial nations were engineered to require continual growth in order to produce jobs, returns on investments, and increasing tax revenues to fund government services. Conclusion 3, which questions whether growth can continue, is therefore deeply subversive. Nearly everyone has an incentive to ignore or avoid it. It's not only objectionable to economic conservatives; it is also abhorrent to many progressives who believe economies must continue to grow so that the working class can get a larger piece of the proverbial pie, and the "underdeveloped" world can improve standards of living.

But ignoring uncomfortable facts seldom makes them go away. Often it just makes matters worse. Back in the 1970s, when environmental limits were first becoming apparent, catastrophe could have been averted with only a relatively small course correction—a gradual tapering of growth and a slow decline in fossil fuel reliance. Now, only a "cold turkey" approach will suffice. If a critical majority of people couldn't be persuaded *then* of the need for a gentle course correction, can they *now* be talked into undertaking deliberate change on a scale and at a speed that might be nearly as traumatic as the climate collision we're trying to avoid?

To be sure, there are those who do accept the message that "growth is over": most are hard-core environmentalists or energy experts. But this is a tiny and poorly organized demographic. If public relations consists of the management of information flowing from an organization to the public, then it surely helps to start with an organization wealthy enough to be able to afford to mount a serious public relations campaign.

This is all quite discouraging, to the point that a fourth conclusion seems justified:

Conclusion 4: Managerial elites will not be persuaded of all three previous conclusions until it is too late to organize a proactive energy transition capable of sustaining the current basic structures of industrial society.

It may be that our inability to voluntarily overcome our reliance on our dominant energy source—fossil fuels—is hardwired into our DNA. Coal, oil, and gas have offered humanity a temporary but enormous energy subsidy. All animals and plants deal with temporary energy subsidies in basically the same way: the pattern is easy to see in the behavior of songbirds visiting the feeder outside my office window. They eat all the seed I've put out for them until the feeder is empty. They don't save some for later or discuss the possible impacts of their current rate of consumption. Yes, we humans have language and therefore the *theoretical* ability to comprehend the likely results of our current collective behavior and alter it accordingly. We exercise this ability in small ways, where the costs of behavior change are relatively trivial—enacting safety standards for new automobiles, for example. But where changing our behavior might entail a significant loss of competitive advantage or an end to economic growth, we tend to act like finches.

Does this mean that society is headed for sudden and utter ruin, that there is nothing we can do to improve our prospects, and that there is absolutely no point in attempting to use public relations to persuade a broad audience of the need for behavior change?

Hardly. As Dmitry Orlov explains in his book *The Five Stages of Collapse*,[4] there are degrees of disorder that can unfold as societies hit the wall. The five stages he identifies are:

1. Financial collapse
2. Commercial collapse
3. Political collapse
4. Social collapse
5. Cultural collapse

In a recent essay he adds a sixth stage, *ecological collapse*.[5] His book (and essay) are worth reading in full, but the takeaway is simple: if you see that the society around you is approaching a period of disintegrative change, do whatever is necessary to stop the process before it reaches stages 4, 5, or (heaven forbid) 6.

Partial success in societal adaptation is better than none at all. Something similar may be true with regard to our public relations efforts: messages underscoring "it's all about energy" and "renewables are the future" are marginally helpful in moving society and its leaders toward greater understanding—even if they fail to point to the inevitability of reductions in energy availability and the realization that "growth is over."

Now add a time dimension. As Everett Rogers pointed out in his book *Diffusion of Innovations*,[6] new ideas and technologies are adopted in stages: first come the innovators, then early adopters. An early majority heralds more widespread acceptance, which spreads even further with the late majority. At the far end of the bell curve come laggards, who resist innovation the longest. While today only a tiny portion of the population accepts that "growth is over," perhaps time and circumstances will change that. Some recent shifts in social values and opinions (such as public acceptance of gay marriage) have

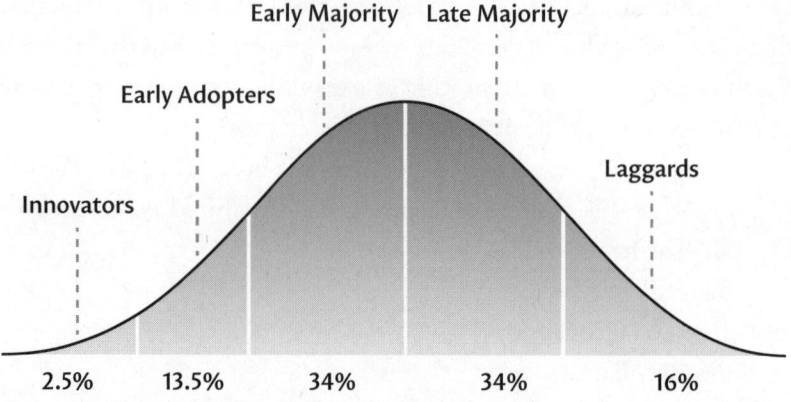

FIGURE 2: The innovation adoption lifecycle

moved from an "early adopter" to "early majority" phase surprisingly rapidly; perhaps energy and climate awareness will likewise eventually overcome what currently appears to be overwhelming resistance.

Another source of inspiration is Donella Meadows's perennially useful paper "Leverage Points: Places to Intervene in a System."[7] Meadows identified 12 leverage points (from constants and parameters, to mindsets and paradigms, to the power to transcend paradigms), which she organized into a hierarchy of relative effectiveness. If we need to change our energy and economic systems profoundly and quickly, we should intervene at the level of paradigms, not regulations and taxes.

Innovators have already teased out the implications of Meadows's paper and acted on them. What's needed, evidently, is an attractive new paradigm that might lead us to proactively reduce our energy consumption. The voluntary simplicity movement blazed that trail back in the 1980s,[8] and the Transition Network has made considerably more headway by organizing whole communities around the task of reducing fossil fuel consumption while relearning preindustrial skills and rebuilding local economies.

Transition also emphasizes building community resilience as an essential strategy in adapting to our emerging energy, economy, and climate reality. This is because (for reasons discussed in the first portion of this essay) we've waited far too long to begin the paradigm shift, so it may not be possible to sustain many of the systems that currently support an industrial mode of societal organization. Shocks are on the way, and we need to bounce rather than shatter.

It's easy to see how elected leaders could help in this vital transformation if they were inclined to do so—for example, by ditching GDP in favor of the genuine progress indicator (GPI) or gross national happiness (GNH) measures. But most policy makers are likely to remain in the "late majority" or even "laggard" categories.[9]

If, like me, you're an innovator or early adopter, there are lots of reasons to feel apprehensive these days. But there is too much at stake to indulge in the luxury of cynicism. Our job is to keep coming up with convincing, well-reasoned, and well-documented arguments for change; attractive PR messages; a compelling new paradigm; and impressive demonstration projects—while opposing further fossil fuel extraction, new roads, and other things that lead toward ecological peril. And we must do it all with as much commitment and vigor as we would if the fate of the world depended on it.

As far as I can tell, it does.

— NOVEMBER 2013

▶ THE PURPOSELY CONFUSING WORLD OF ENERGY POLITICS

LIFE OFTEN PRESENTS US WITH PARADOXES, BUT SELDOM SO blatant or consequential as the following. Read this sentence slowly: Today it is especially difficult for most people to understand our perilous global energy situation, precisely *because* it has never been more important to do so. Got that? No? Okay, let me explain. I must begin by briefly retracing developments in a seemingly unrelated field—climate science.

Once upon a time, the idea that Earth's climate could be changing due to human-caused carbon dioxide emissions was just a lonely, unpopular scientific hypothesis. Through years that stretched to decades, researchers patiently gathered troves of evidence to test that hypothesis. The great majority of evidence collected tended to confirm the notion that rising atmospheric carbon dioxide (and other greenhouse gas) levels raise average global temperatures and provoke an increase in extreme weather events. Nearly all climate scientists were gradually persuaded of the correctness of the global warming hypothesis.

But a funny thing happened along the way. Clearly, if the climate is changing rapidly and dramatically as a result of human action, and if climate change (of the scale and speed that's anticipated) is likely to undermine ecosystems and economies, then it stands to reason that humans should stop emitting so much carbon dioxide. In practical effect, this would mean dramatically reducing our burning of fossil fuels—the main drivers of economic growth since the beginning of the Industrial Revolution.

Some business-friendly folks with political connections soon became alarmed at both the policy implications of—and the likely short-term economic fallout from—the way climate science was developing, and decided to do everything they could to question, denigrate, and deny the climate change hypothesis. Their effort succeeded: Especially in the United States, belief in climate change now aligns fairly closely with political affiliation. Most elected Democrats agree that the issue is real and important, and most of their Republican counterparts are skeptical. Lacking bipartisan support, legislative climate policy has languished.

From a policy standpoint, climate change is effectively an energy issue, since reducing carbon emissions will require a nearly complete revamping of our energy systems. Energy is, by definition, humanity's most basic source of power, and since politics is a contest over power (albeit *social* power), it should not be surprising that energy is politically contested. A politician's most basic tools are power and persuasion, and the ability to frame issues. And the tactics of political argument inevitably range well beyond logic and critical thinking. Therefore politicians can and often do make it harder for people to understand energy issues than would be the case if accurate, unbiased information were freely available.

So here is the reason for the paradox stated in the first paragraph: As energy issues become more critically important to society's economic and ecological survival, they become more politically contested; and as a result, they tend to become obscured by a fog of exaggeration, half-truth, omission, and outright prevarication.

How does one cut through this fog to gain a more accurate view of what's happening in our society's vital energy supply-and-support systems? It's helpful to start by understanding the positions and motives of the political actors. For the sake of argument, I will caricature two political positions. Let's personify them as Politician A and Politician B.

Politician A has for many years sided with big business, and specifically with the fossil fuel industry in all energy disputes. She sees coal, oil, and natural gas as gifts of nature to be used by humanity to produce as much wealth as possible, as quickly as possible. She asserts that there are sufficient supplies of these fuels to meet the needs of future generations, even if we use them at rapidly increasing rates. When coal, oil, and gas do eventually start to run out, Politician A says we can always turn to nuclear energy. In her view, the harvesting and burning of fossil fuels can be accomplished with few incidental environmental problems, and fossil fuel companies can be trusted to use the safest methods available. And if Earth's climate is indeed changing, she says, this is not due to the burning of fossil fuels; therefore, policies meant to cut fossil fuel consumption are unnecessary and economically damaging. Finally, she says renewable energy sources should not be subsidized by government, but should stand or fall according to their own economic merits.

Politician B regards oil, coal, and natural gas as polluting substances, and society's addiction to them as shameful. He thinks oil prices are high because petroleum companies gouge their customers; nuclear energy is too dangerous to contemplate; and renewable energy sources are benign (with supplies of sunlight and wind vastly exceeding our energy needs). To hear him tell it, the only reason solar and wind still supply such a small percentage of our total energy is that fossil fuel companies are politically powerful, benefiting from generous, often hidden, government subsidies. Government should cut those subsidies and support renewable energy instead. He believes climate change is a serious problem, and to mitigate it we should put a price on carbon emissions. If we do, Politician B says, renewable energy industries will grow rapidly, creating jobs and boosting the economy.

Who is right? Well, this should be easy to determine. Just ignore the foaming rhetoric and focus on research findings. But in reality that's not easy at all, because research is itself often politicized. Studies can be designed from the outset to give results that are friendly to the preconceptions and prejudices of one partisan group or another.

For example, there are studies that appear to show that the oil and natural gas production technique known as hydraulic fracturing (or "fracking") is safe for the environment.[1] With research in hand, industry representatives calmly inform us that there have been *no* confirmed instances of fracking fluids contaminating water tables. The implication: environmentalists who complain about the dangers of fracking simply don't know what they're talking about.

However, there are indeed many documented instances of water pollution associated with fracking,[2] though technically most of these have resulted from the improper disposal of wastewater produced once hydraulic fracturing per se is finished, rather than from the process itself. Further, industry-funded studies of fracking typically focus on sites where best practices are in place and equipment is working as designed—the ideal scenario. In the messy real world, well casings sometimes fail, operators cut corners, and equipment occasionally malfunctions. (For their part, environmentalists point to peer-reviewed studies showing air, water, and human health problems associated with actual fracking operations.)[3]

So, depending on your prior beliefs, you can often choose research findings to support them—even if the studies you are citing are actually highly misleading.

Renewable energy is just as contentious. Mark Jacobson, professor of environmental engineering at Stanford University, has coauthored a series of reports and scientific papers arguing that solar, wind, and hydropower could provide 100 percent of world energy by 2030.[4] Clearly, Jacobson's work supports Politician B's political narrative by showing that the climate problem can be solved with little or no economic sacrifice. If Jacobson is right, then it is only the fossil fuel companies and their supporters that stand in the way of a solution to our environmental (and economic) problems. The Sierra Club and prominent Hollywood stars have latched onto Jacobson's work and promote it enthusiastically.

However, Jacobson's publications have provoked thoughtful criticism, some of it from supporters of renewable energy, who argue that his "100 percent renewables by 2030" scenario ignores hidden costs, land use and environmental problems, and grid limits.[5] Jacobson has replied to his critics, well, energetically.[6]

At the other end of the opinion spectrum on renewable energy is Gail Tverberg, an actuary by training and profession (and no shill for the fossil fuel industry), whose analysis suggests that the more solar and wind generating capacity we build, the worse off we are from an economic point of view.[7] Her conclusion flatly contradicts that of an influential report by Swiss think tank SolaVis, which aims to show that the more renewables we build, the more money we'll save.[8] Ecologist Charles Hall has determined that the ratio of energy returned to energy invested in capturing solar energy with photovoltaic (PV) panels is too low to support an industrial economy.[9] Meanwhile the solar industry claims that PV can provide *all* of society's power needs.[10] An article in the journal *Energy Policy* claims global wind capacity may have been seriously overestimated.[11] An article in the journal *Nature* says this may not be the case.[12]

In sum, if you're looking for quick and simple answers to questions about how much renewables can do for us, at what price, and over what time frame, forget it! These questions are far from being settled.

There's a saying: For every PhD, there is an equal and opposite PhD. Does this mean science is useless, and objective reality is whatever you want it to be? Of course not. However, politics and cultural bias can and do muddy the process and results of scientific research.

All of this is inevitable; it's human nature. We'll sort through the confusion, given time and the hard knocks that inevitably come when preconceptions veer too far from the facts. However, if the more worrisome implications of climate science are right, we may not have a lot of time for sorting, and our knocks may be very hard indeed.

⋘⋙

Here's a corollary to my thesis: *Political prejudices tend to blind us to facts that fail to fit any conventional political agendas.* All political narratives need a villain and a (potential) happy ending. While Politicians A and B might point to different villains (government bureaucrats and regulators on one hand, oil companies on the other), they both envision the same happy ending: economic growth, though it is to be achieved by contrasting means. If a fact doesn't fit one of these two narratives, the offended politician tends to ignore it (or attempt to deny it). If it doesn't fit either narrative, nearly everyone ignores it.

Here's a fact that apparently fails to comfortably fit into either political narrative: *The energy and financial returns on fossil fuel extraction are declining—fast.* The top five oil majors (ExxonMobil, BP, Shell, Chevron, and Total) have seen their aggregate production fall by more than 25 percent over the past 12 years—but it's not for lack of effort.[13] Drilling rates have doubled. Rates of capital investment in exploration and production have likewise doubled.[14] Oil prices have quadrupled. Yet actual global rates of production for regular crude oil have flattened, and all new production has come from expensive unconventional sources such as tar sands, tight oil, and deepwater oil.[15] The fossil fuel industry hates to admit to facts like this that investors find scary—especially now, as the industry needs investors to pony up ever-larger bets to pay for ever-more-extreme production projects.

In the past few years, high oil prices have provided the incentive for small, highly leveraged, and risk-friendly companies to go after

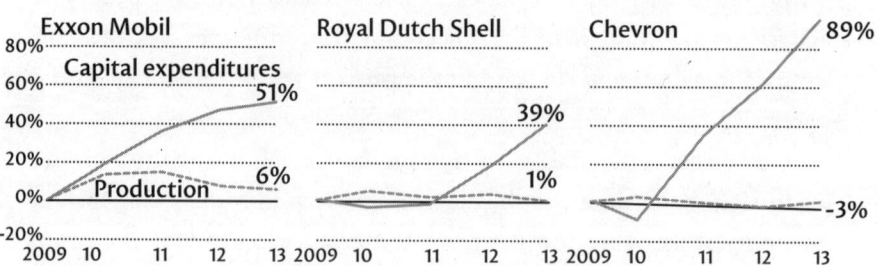

FIGURE 3: A Costly Quest. Source: Daniel Gilbert and Justin Sheck, "Big Oil Companies Struggle to Justify Soaring Project Costs," the *Wall Street Journal*, January 28, 2014.

some of the last, worst oil and gas production prospects in North America—formations known to geologists as "source rocks," which require operators to use horizontal drilling and fracking technology to free up trapped hydrocarbons. The ratio of energy returned to energy invested in producing shale gas and tight oil from these formations is minimal. While US oil and gas production rates have temporarily spiked, all signs indicate that this will be a brief boom[16] that will not change the overall situation significantly: society is reaching the point of diminishing returns with regard to the economic benefits of fossil fuel extraction.

And what about our imaginary politicians? Politician A wouldn't want to talk about any of this for fairly obvious reasons. But strangely, Politician B likely would avoid the subject too: while he might portray the petroleum industry as an ogre, his narrative requires it to be a *powerful* ogre. Also, he probably doesn't like to think that high gasoline prices might be caused by oil depletion rather than the simple greed of the petroleum barons. Motives can be complicated; perhaps both feel the patriotic urge to cheer domestic energy production, regardless of its source and in spite of evidence of declining returns on investment. Perhaps both understand that declining energy returns imply really bad news for the economy, regardless of which party is in power. In any case, mum's the word.

Some facts seem to fit one narrative or the other but, when combined, point to a reality that undermines both narratives. *What if climate change is an even worse problem than most of us assume, and there is no realistic way to deal seriously with it and still have economic growth?*

In the real world of US politics, many Democrats would agree with the first part of the sentence, many Republicans with the second. Yet both parties would flee from endorsing the statement as a whole. Nevertheless, this seems to be where the data are driving us. Actual climate impacts have consistently outpaced the worst-case forecasts issued by the UN's International Panel on Climate Change (IPCC) for the past two decades.[17] That means curbing carbon emissions is even more urgent than almost anyone previously thought. The math has changed. At this point, the rate of reduction in fossil fuel consumption required in order to avert catastrophic climate change may be higher, possibly much higher, than the realistically possible rate of replacement with energy from alternative sources. Climatologist Kevin Anderson of the UK-based Tyndall Centre figures that industrial nations need to cut carbon emissions by up to ten percent per year to avert catastrophe, and that such a rapid reduction would be "incompatible with economic growth."[18] What if he's right?

The problem of transitioning quickly away from fossil fuels while maintaining economic growth is exacerbated by the unique characteristics of different energy sources.

Here's just one example of the difficulty of replacing oil while maintaining economic growth. Oil is the perfect transport fuel: it stores a lot of energy per unit of weight and volume. Electric batteries can't match its performance. Plug-in electric vehicles exist, of course (though less than one percent of new vehicles sold in the United States in 2013 were plug-in electrics[19]), but batteries cannot propel airliners or long-haul, eighteen-wheel truck rigs. Yet the trucking and airline industries just happen to be significant components of our economy; can we abandon or significantly downsize them and grow the economy as we do so?

What about non-transport replacements for fossil fuels? Well, both nuclear power stations and renewable energy systems have high up-front investment costs. If you factor in *all* the financial and energy costs (something the solar, wind, and nuclear industries are reluctant to do), their payback time is often measured in decades. Thus there seems to be no realistic way to bootstrap the energy transition (for example, by using the power from solar panels to build more solar panels) while continuing to provide enough energy to keep the rest of the economy expanding. In effect, to maintain growth, the energy transition would have to be subsidized by fossil fuels—which would largely defeat the purpose of the exercise.

Business-friendly politicians seem to intuitively get much of this, and this knowledge helps fuel their continued infatuation with oil, coal, and natural gas—despite the increasing *economic* problems (even if we disregard the environmental problems) with these fuels. But these folks' way of dealing with this conundrum is simply to deny that climate change is a real issue. That strategy may work for their supporters in the fossil fuel industries, but it does nothing to avert the worsening real-world crises of extreme temperature events, droughts, floods, and storms—and their knock-on impacts on agriculture, economies, and governments.

So those on the political left may be correct in saying that climate change is the equivalent of a civilization-killing asteroid, while those on the political right may be correct in thinking that policies designed to shrink carbon emissions will shrink the economy as well. Everybody gets to be correct—but nobody gets a happy ending (at least as currently envisioned).

That's because nearly every politician wants growth, or at least recognizes the need to clamor for growth in order to be electable. Because growth, after all, is how we currently define our collective, national happy ending. So whenever facts lead toward the conclusion that more growth may not be possible *even if our party gets its way,* those facts quickly get swept under the nearest carpet.

Masking reality with political rhetoric leads to delays in doing what is necessary—making the best of the choices actually available to us. We and our political "leaders" continue to deny and pretend, walking blindly toward environmental and economic peril.

How can we work effectively in a politically polarized environment? Hyper-partisanship is a problem in approving judicial appointees and passing budgets, and failure to do these things can have serious consequences. But when it comes to energy and climate, the scale of what is at stake runs straight off the charts. The decisions that need to be made on energy and climate—and soon (ideally, 20 years ago!)—may well determine whether civilization survives. The absence of decisive action will imperil literally everything we care about.

Energy is complicated, and there can be legitimate disagreements about our options and how vigorously to pursue them. But the status quo is not working.

I've struggled to find a hopeful takeaway message with which to end this essay.

Should I appeal to colleagues who write about energy, pleading with them to frame discussions in ways that aren't merely feeding red meat to their already far-too-polarized audiences, encouraging them to tell readers uncomfortable truths that don't fit partisan narratives? I could, but how many energy analysts are honestly willing to examine their preconceptions?

Perhaps it's fitting that this essay leaves both author and readers unsettled and uncomfortable. Discomfort can sometimes be conducive to creativity and action. There may be no solutions to the political problems I've outlined. But even in the absence of solutions there can still be better adaptive behaviors, and judo-like strategies that achieve desired outcomes—ones that could conceivably turn the tide on intractable global problems such as climate change—without directly confronting existing societal power structures. These behaviors and strategies can be undertaken even at the household scale, but we're likely to achieve much more if we collaborate, doing what we can locally while using global communications to compare notes and share our successes and challenges.

— FEBRUARY 2014

▶ THE BRIEF, TRAGIC REIGN OF CONSUMERISM

— AND THE BIRTH OF A HAPPY ALTERNATIVE

You and I consume; we are consumers. The global economy is set up to enable us to do what we innately want to do—buy, use, discard, and buy some more. If we do our job well, the economy thrives; if for some reason we fail at our task, the economy falters. The model of economic existence just described is reinforced in the business pages of every newspaper, and in the daily reportage of nearly every financial news service, and it has a familiar name: *consumerism*.

Consumerism has a history, but not a long one. True, humans—like all other animals—are consumers in the most basic sense, in that we must eat to live. Further, we have been making weapons, ornaments, clothing, utensils, toys, and musical instruments for tens of thousands of years, and commerce has likewise been with us for untold millennia.

What's new is the project of organizing an entire society around *the necessity for ever-increasing rates of personal consumption.*

This Is How It Happened

Consumerism arose from a unique historic milieu. In the early 20th century, a temporary abundance of cheap, concentrated, storable, and portable energy in the form of fossil fuels enabled a dramatic increase in the rate and scope of resource extraction (via powered mining equipment, chain saws, tractors, powered fishing boats, and more). Coupled with powered assembly lines and the use of petrochemicals, cheap fossil energy also permitted a vast expansion in the manufacture of a widening array of commercial products. This resulted in a serious economic problem known as *overproduction* (too many goods chasing too few buyers), which would eventually contribute to the Great Depression of the 1930s.

Industrialists found a solution. How they did so is detailed in a book that deserves renewed attention: *Captains of Consciousness* by social historian Stuart Ewen (1976).[1] In it, Ewen traces the rapid, massive growth of the advertising industry during the 20th century, as well as its extraordinary social and political impacts (if you really want to understand *Mad Men*, start here). He argues that "Consumerism, the mass participation in the values of the mass-industrial market... emerged in the 1920s not as a smooth progression from earlier and less 'developed' patterns of consumption, but rather as an aggressive device of corporate survival."

In a later book, *PR!* (1996),[2] Ewen recounts how, during the 1930s, the US-based National Association of Manufacturers enlisted a team of advertisers, marketers, and psychologists to formulate a strategy to counter government efforts to plan and manage the economy in the wake of the Depression. They proposed a massive, ongoing ad campaign to equate consumerism with "The American Way." *Progress* would henceforth be framed entirely in economic terms, as the fruit of manufacturers' ingenuity. Americans were to be referred to in public discourse (newspapers, magazines, radio) as *consumers*, and were to be reminded at every opportunity of their duty to contribute to the economy by purchasing factory-made products, as directed by increasingly sophisticated and ubiquitous advertising cues.

While advertising was an essential prop to consumerism, by itself it was incapable of stoking sufficient demand to soak up all the goods rolling off assembly lines. In the early years of the last century Americans were accustomed to paying cash for their purchases. But then along came automobiles: not many people could afford to pay for one outright, yet nearly everybody wanted one. In addition to being talked into desiring more products, consumers had to be enabled to purchase more of them than they could immediately pay for; hence the widespread deployment of time payments and other forms of consumer credit. With credit, households could *consume now and pay later*. Consumers took on more debt, the financial industry mushroomed, and manufacturers sold more products.

Though consumerism began as a project organized by corporate America, government at all levels swiftly lent its support. When citizens spent more on consumer goods, sales tax and income tax revenues tended to swell. After World War II, government advocacy of increased consumer spending was formalized with the adoption of gross domestic product (GDP) as the nation's primary measure of economic success, and with the increasing use of the term *consumer* by government agencies.

By the 1950s, consumerism was thoroughly interwoven in the fabric of American society. In 1955, economist Victor Lebow would epitomize the new status quo, writing in the *Journal of Retailing*: "Our enormously productive economy demands that we make consumption our way of life, that we convert the buying and use of goods into rituals, that we seek our spiritual satisfaction and our ego satisfaction in consumption. We need things consumed, burned up, worn out, replaced and discarded at an ever-increasing rate."

What Could Possibly Go Wrong?

Meanwhile critics had identified a couple of serious problems with consumerism.

First problem: Consumerism, according to the naysayers, warps human values. Way back in 1899, when consumerism was barely a glimmer in advertisers' neurons, economist Thorstein Veblen asserted in his widely cited book *The Theory of the Leisure Class*[3] that there exists a fundamental split in society between those who work and those who exploit the work of others; as societies evolve, the latter come to constitute a "leisure class" that engages in "conspicuous consumption." Veblen saw mass production as a way to universalize the trappings of leisure so the owning class could engage workers in an endless pursuit of status symbols, thus deflecting workers' attention from society's increasingly unequal distribution of wealth and their own political impotence. Later critics of consumerism included German historian Oswald Spengler, who wrote that "Life in America is exclusively economic in structure and lacks depth"; Mohandas Gandhi, who regarded a simple life free from possessions as morally ennobling; and Scott and Helen Nearing, authors of *Living the Good Life*[4] and pioneers of the back-to-the-land movement. Social critics of consumerism like Duane Elgin, Juliet Schor, Helena Norberg-Hodge, and Vicki Robin have argued that relationships with products or brand names are dysfunctional substitutes for healthy human relationships and that consumer choice is a soporific stand-in for genuine democracy.

A second and more crucial problem with consumerism, say the critics, has to do with resource limits. Environmental scientists assert that, regardless of whether it is socially desirable, consumerism is physically impossible to maintain in the long run. The math is simple: even if consumption only grows a fraction of one percent every year, all of Earth's resources will eventually be used up. The consumer economy also produces an unending variety of wastes, of which water, air, and soil can absorb only so much before planetary life-support systems begin unraveling.

In his 1954 book *The Challenge of Man's Future*,[5] physicist Harrison Brown envisioned devastating social and environmental consequences from the relentless growth of human population and resource consumption; he even managed to foresee the current climate crisis. A few years later a team of researchers at MIT began using a computer to model likely future scenarios ensuing from population expansion, consumption growth, and environmental decline. In the computer's "standard run" scenario, continued growth led to a global economic collapse in the mid-21st century. That project's findings were documented in the pivotal 1972 book *Limits to Growth*,[6] which received blistering reviews from mainstream economists but has since been vindicated by independent retrospective analysis.[7]

More recently, E. F. Schumacher, Herman Daly, William Rees, and other advocates of ecological economics[8] have pointed out that the consumer economy treats Earth's irreplaceable capital (natural resources) as if it were income—an obvious theoretical error with potentially catastrophic real-world results.

A Self-reinforcing System

Often these critiques have led to a simple personal prescription: If buying ever more stuff is bad for the environment and turns us into vapid mall drones, then it's up to each of us to rein in our consumptive habits. Buy nothing! Reuse! Recycle! Share!

Yet treating consumerism as though it were merely an individual proclivity rather than a complex, interdependent system with financial, governmental, and commercial components is both wrong and mostly ineffectual. Consider this simple thought experiment: What would happen if *everyone* were to suddenly embrace a Gandhian ethic of voluntary simplicity? Commerce would contract; jobs would vanish; pension funds would lose value; tax revenues would shrivel, and so would government services. Absent sweeping structural changes to government and the economy, the result would be a deep, long-lasting economic depression.

This is not to say that personal efforts toward voluntary simplicity have no benefit—they do, for the individual and her circle of associates. However, the *system* of consumerism can only be altered or replaced through *systemic* action. Yet this is hampered by the fact that consumerism has become self-reinforcing: those with significant roles in the system who try to rein it in get whacked, while those who help it expand get stroked. Nearly everybody wants an economy with more jobs and higher returns on investments, so for most people, the incentive to shut up and get with the program is overwhelming. Arguments against consumerism may be rationally irrefutable, but few people stop to think about them.

If mere persuasion could dismantle consumerism or replace it with something better, it would have done so by now.

Crisis Time

Still, as the critics have insisted all along, consumerism as a system cannot continue indefinitely; it contains the seeds of its own demise. And the natural constraints to consumerism—fossil fuel limits, environmental sink limits (leading to climate change, ocean acidification, and other pollution dilemmas), and debt limits—appear to be well within sight. While there may be short-term ways of pushing back against these limits (unconventional oil and gas, geoengineering, quantitative easing), there is no way around them. Consumerism is inherently doomed. But since consumerism now effectively *is* the economy (70 percent of US GDP comes from consumer spending), when it goes down the economy goes too.

A train wreck is foreseeable. No one knows exactly when the impact will occur or precisely how bad it will be. But it is possible to say with some confidence that this wreck will manifest itself as an economic depression accompanied by a series of worsening environmental disasters and possibly wars and revolutions. This should be news to nobody by now, as recent government and UN reports spin out the scenarios in ever grimmer detail: rising sea levels, waves of environmental refugees, droughts, floods, famines, and collapsing economies.[9]

Indeed, looking at what's happened since the start of the global economic crisis in 2007, it's likely the impact has already commenced—though it is happening in agonizingly slow motion as the system fights to maintain itself.

The Happy Alternative

It is not too soon to wonder what comes after consumerism. If there is good news to be gleaned from the story just told, it is that this mode of economic existence is not biologically determined. Consumerism arose from a certain set of circumstances; as circumstances change, other economic arrangements will offer adaptive advantages.

If we have some idea of the circumstances that are likely to emerge in the decades ahead, we may get some clues to what those alternative arrangements may look like. As we've already seen, the consumerist economy of the 20th century was driven by cheap energy and over-production. All signs suggest the new century will be shaped by energy limits, environmental sink limits, and debt limits—and therefore by declining production per capita. Under these circumstances, policy makers will surely strive to provide a *sufficiency* economy. But how do we get from a consumerist economy to a sufficiency economy?

Perhaps the most promising clue comes from the emerging happiness movement. Since the 1970s, the tiny Himalayan kingdom of Bhutan has experimented with gross national happiness (GNH)[10] as a measure of economic success; in 2012, the country convened a meeting at the United Nations to advocate widespread international adoption of GNH. Concurrently, the New Economics Foundation of Britain has begun publishing an annually updated Happy Planet Index (HPI),[11] which ranks nations by the self-reported levels of happiness of their citizens and by the size of their ecological footprints.

The point of GNH and HPI is to measure a country's success more by how people feel about their lives and circumstances and less by consumption (which is what GDP does, in effect). Happiness metrics are kryptonite to consumerism, which has been shown time and again to make people *less* satisfied with the circumstances of their lives. A wholesale official adoption of GNH or HPI by the world's nations would ultimately lead to a profound shuffling of priorities. Governments would have to promote policies that lead to more sharing, more equity, more transparency, and more citizen participation in governance, since it is these sorts of things that tend to push happiness scores higher.

The guardians of the consumer economy are not stupid. They will not permit the wholesale introduction of happiness metrics absent necessity. But, as we've seen, necessity is coming. As the current consumer economy frays and sputters, policy makers will need increasingly to find ways to pacify the multitudes and give them some sense of direction. Beyond a certain point, promises of a return to the days of carefree shopping will ring hollow.

Happiness indices may constitute a collective adaptation that could ease the transition from one economic mode to the next, reducing the trauma that will likely accompany the demise of consumerism. GNH or HPI may be effective packages in which to "sell" sufficiency to policy makers and citizens; they may also be pathways to a genuinely superior mode of human existence.

— JULY 2013

▶ FINGERS IN THE DIKE

THE 19TH-CENTURY NOVEL *HANS BRINKER, OR THE SILVER Skates* by American author Mary Mapes Dodge features a brief story-within-a-story that has become better known in popular culture than the book itself. It's the tale of a Dutch boy (in the novel he's called simply "The Hero of Haarlem") who saves his community by jamming his finger into a leaking levee. The boy stays put, enduring the elements, until villagers find him and fix the leak. His courageous action in holding back potential floodwaters has become celebrated in children's literature and art, to the point where it serves as a convenient metaphor.

Here in the early 21st century there are three dams about to break, and in each case a calamity is being postponed—though not, in these cases, by the heroic digits of fictitious Dutch children.

A grasp of the status of these three delayed disasters, and what's putting them off, may help us to navigate waters that now rise slowly, though soon perhaps in torrents.

1. Unconventional Fuels and Production Methods

I've written so much on the subject of peak oil, and some of it so recently,[1] that it would be redundant to go into much detail here on that score. Suffice it to say that world conventional crude oil production has been flat-to-declining since about 2005. Declines of output from the world's supergiant oilfields will steepen in the years ahead. Petroleum is essential to the world economy and there is no ready and sufficient substitute. The potential consequences of peak oil include prolonged economic crisis and resource wars.

Producers of unconventional liquid fuels—tar sands, tight oil, and deepwater oil—are playing the role of the Dutch boy in the energy world, though their motives may not be quite so altruistic. With unconventional sources included in the total, world petroleum production has grown somewhat in recent years, but oil prices are hovering at near-record levels because unconventionals are expensive to produce. The oil industry has successfully used this meager success as a public relations tool, arguing that it can continue pulling rabbits out of hats for as long as needed and that policy makers therefore need do nothing to prepare society for a peak-oil future. In fact, world oil markets are depending almost entirely on continued increases in production from the United States—all of which must come from fracked, horizontally drilled wells that decline rapidly—to keep supplies steady.[2] Even the US Energy Information Administration recognizes that the US tight oil boom will be history by the end of the current decade—though the official forecast shows production levels gently drifting thereafter when in all likelihood they will plummet given the spectacular per-well decline rates of the current top-producing plays, the Bakken and Eagle Ford formations.[3]

Is there another Dutch boy waiting, finger ready? At one point the largest tight oil deposits in the United States were said to be in California's Monterey formation; the EIA released a report in 2011 forecasting that the Monterey would ultimately yield 15.4 billion barrels of crude, about two-thirds of the country's total tight oil reserves. However, subsequent analysis undertaken by my colleague David Hughes at Post Carbon Institute significantly dampened such expectations; and sure enough, in mid-2014 the EIA gutted the Monterey forecast by 96 percent to a measly 600 million barrels.[4] Tight oil deposits in other countries will take longer to develop than those in the United States and will present more technical and especially political challenges (fossil fuel extraction can be very lucrative for property owners in the United States, but in most other countries it's the government that profits from extracting or selling access to underground resources). Other unconventionals, like extra-heavy oil in Venezuela and kerogen (also known as "oil shale," and not to be confused with shale oil) in the American West, will be even slower and more expensive to produce—if they're ever tapped to any significant extent (Shell abandoned its kerogen research operations in 2013 without any prospect of eventual profitability).[5]

Bottom line: the recent, ongoing "new normal" of high but stable oil prices may last another few years; after that, oil supplies will become much more problematic, and prices are anybody's guess. The dam is weakening. Have your hip boots and waders ready.

2. Quantitative Easing

The financial crash of 2008, bad as it was, should really be thought of as merely a symptom of a more pervasive, profound, and ongoing shift in the entire global economy. Our growth-based, fossil-fueled economic system is colliding with foreseeable energy and debt limits.[6] We constructed our existing financial system during a historic period of anomalous rapid growth; without further growth in manufacturing, transport, and trade, the pyramid of credit and leverage built by investors during recent decades is likely to implode. We got just a taste of what might be in store with the Lehman and AIG failures.

Some who understood the system's vulnerability early on, and who warned that a crash was imminent, forecast a rapid collapse of the entire economy. Each year from 2008 up to the present, these commentators have insisted that in a matter of months we'll see bread lines, shuttered banks, and riots in the streets. Riots and bank failures have indeed shown up in Greece, but here in the United States (and Britain, Germany, China, Canada, Australia…the list continues) economic life goes on. In the United States, pre-crash norms in

employment, household income, and house values have not fully returned, but neither has the sky fallen. Most economists say the nation
is in the midst of a "fragile recovery."

Why no collapse? Governments and central banks have inserted
fingers in financial levees. Most notably, the Federal Reserve rushed
to keep crisis at bay by purchasing tens of billions of dollars in US
Treasury bonds each month, year after year, using money created
out of thin air at the moment of purchase. This has enabled the federal government to borrow at low interest rates; it also props up the
American financial industry. Indeed, virtually all of the Fed's money
has stayed within financial circles;[7] that's a big reason why the richest
Americans have gotten much richer in the past few years, while most
regular folks are treading water at best.[8]

This go-for-broke policy is called quantitative easing (QE); it's
poorly understood by the general public and provokes strong reac-
tions from many economists. Some think QE must lead to hyperinflation (it hasn't so far, and it's been going on since late 2008). Others
think that, in principle, it could be used (if differently organized and
applied) to solve all our debt problems.[9]

Be that as it may, what has the too-big-to-fail, too-greedy-not-to
financial system done with the Fed's trillions in free money? Blown
another stock market bubble and piled up more leveraged bets. No
one knows when the latest bubble will pop, but when it does the ensuing crisis may be much worse than that of 2008. Will central banks
then be able to jam more fingers into the leaky levee? Will they have
enough fingers?

3. Global Warming "Pause"

The threat of climate change needs no introduction—it's the mother
of all impending environmental crises. And we are already seeing serious impacts, including superstorms, droughts, and the melting of the
north polar ice cap. Nevertheless, it's all not as bad as it might be, were
it not for the fact that the warming of Earth's surface air temperatures
has slowed since 1998 (which was an anomalously hot year).[10]

Climate change deniers have seized upon evidence of this "pause" to argue that global warming has essentially stopped.[11] After all, if the greenhouse-gas-laden atmosphere were in fact trapping more heat, where could all that heat be hiding?

Turns out, very little of Earth's trapped heat warms the atmosphere and land surface; most of it (more than 90 percent) is absorbed by the oceans. Part of the explanation for the slowdown in surface warming lies in the heating of deep ocean waters.[12] Global warming hasn't really "paused"; it's just gone to the depths. At the same time, there has been a recent downswing in the Pacific Ocean's natural temperature cycle, which has also correlated with a cluster of La Niña years (usually associated with a cooling of ocean surface waters). This temperature cycle masks the underlying warming trend.[13] So it appears that, for now at least, Mother Earth herself is playing "The Hero of Haarlem."

There's no way to know how long this current cool cycle will last, though the previous Pacific cool phase, which started in the 1940s, continued for about 30 years. If the present cycle is of the same duration, then in about 15 years much of the heat currently being dumped in deep oceans may begin instead to remain in the atmosphere. At that point we will likely see unprecedented rates of climate warming, and far worse episodes of extreme weather.[14]

The fact that climate change is complex and nonlinear makes it hard to communicate the urgency of the problem even to scientifically literate audiences. Arthur Petersen, chief scientist at the Netherlands Environmental Assessment Agency and part of the Dutch delegation that reviewed the latest IPCC report,[15] was quoted by the BBC as saying: "It is a major feat that we have been able to produce such a document which is such an adequate assessment of the science. That being said, it is virtually unreadable!"[16]

Making the Most of Borrowed Time

In the story of the Dutch boy, adults in the village eventually find the brave child and repair the dike. But for the three leaky systems discussed above, the necessary repairs aren't being made. Most governments aren't rapidly developing renewable energy and public transport infrastructure; instead, they're spending their money on building more roads. The financial system is not being downsized and regulated; it's being propped up and inflated. Fossil fuel use is not being discouraged with meaningful carbon taxes (except in a very few countries); instead, oil and gas industries are subsidized.

The folks in charge will probably continue to buy as much time as they can, for as long as they can, even if doing so makes the situation worse in the long run. Nature is less predictable: humans cannot control the duration of the global warming "pause."

The phrase "living on borrowed time" inevitably comes to mind, with its implication of impending doom. Yet we simply don't know how serious the impacts of these delayed crises will be within a humanly meaningful timeframe—say, the next ten or twenty years. Doom is possible, but nature, central banks, and crafty drillers may yet conspire to maintain the appearance of normalcy in the eyes of at least some of the population even as the waters rise around our ankles. No collapse here, folks; just keep shopping.

It's hard to know what attitude to adopt with regard to these things. Given that delays will likely make matters worse when the dam does break, and that fundamental repairs aren't being undertaken, should we therefore say, "Bring on the crisis, let's get it over with?" If that *is* our stance, then what might be done to accelerate events? Our oil-supply situation could be hastened slightly toward crisis if, for example, the federal government stopped expanding pipelines (like the Keystone XL) meant to service tar sands mining in Alberta, or state governments enacted tighter restrictions on hydraulic fracturing ("fracking") for tight oil (there's no "bring-on-the-crisis" upside to decisions *in favor* of pipelines or fracking—these will worsen the climate dilemma without doing anything to end the global warming "pause"). Maybe causing a US government default would usher in the next chapter of global financial Armageddon: that's entirely within the capabilities of at least a few people, and they seemed to do a very good job of marching us toward the brink back in 2012–13, when Congress very nearly caused a default on Federal debt obligations.

Or shall we simply enjoy our remaining days of "normal" life? Spend time at the beach. Learn to play a musical instrument. See friends and family. Those are perfectly understandable and legitimate ways of whiling away borrowed time.

Here's a thought: How about using whatever interval we have— whether it turns out to be weeks or decades—to build community resilience? Get to know your neighbors. Plan next season's garden. Join efforts to create a community-run renewable energy utility company. Buy from local farmers. Put your savings in the local credit union. Take a Transition Launch! training course.[17]

If we do these things now, then when fingers can no longer plug leaks the ensuing mess may be far less daunting. And in the meantime we may enjoy substantial social and psychological benefits from living in a way that's more localized and communitarian.

If that's your choice, you'd better get going. There's no telling how much time we have.

— OCTOBER 2013

8

▶ YOUR POST-PETROLEUM FUTURE

(A COMMENCEMENT ADDRESS)

Thanks to Students for a Just and Stable Future of Worcester Polytechnic Institute for making this occasion possible, and for inviting me to speak to you today. To the students: Your courage and persistence are admirable. You are our hope for the future.

Thanks also to President Berkey and the rest of the WPI administration for making this space available and for their willingness to listen to students' concerns.

The reason for this "alternative" commencement speech is that some students were upset to learn that their college had invited Rex Tillerson, the CEO of ExxonMobil, to bestow a message of blessing upon their graduation. As Linnea Palmer Paton put it in a letter to WPI President Berkey, "[W]e, as conscientious members of the WPI community and proud members of the Class of 2011, will not give [the Exxon CEO] the honor of imparting...his well-wishes...for our futures...when he is largely responsible for undermining them."

I think Linnea got it exactly right. ExxonMobil is inviting you to take your place in a fossil-fueled 21st century. But I would argue that Exxon's vision of the future is actually just a forward projection from our collective rearview mirror. Despite its hi-tech gadgetry, the oil industry is a relic of the days of the *Beverly Hillbillies*. This fossil-fueled sitcom of a world that we all find ourselves trapped within may on the surface appear to be characterized by smiley-faced happy motoring, but at its core it is monstrous and grotesque. It is a zombie energy economy.

Of course, we all use petroleum and natural gas in countless ways and on a daily basis. These are amazing substances: they are energy-dense and chemically useful, and they yield enormous economic benefit. America started out with vast reserves of oil and gas, and they helped make our nation the richest and most powerful country in the world.

But oil and gas are finite resources, so it was clear from the start that, as we extracted and burned them, we were in effect stealing from the future. In the early days, the quantities of these fuels available seemed so enormous that depletion posed only a theoretical limit to consumption. We knew we would eventually empty the tanks of Earth's hydrocarbon reserves, but that was a problem for our great-great-grandkids to worry about. Yet US oil production started declining in 1970, despite huge discoveries in Alaska and the Gulf of Mexico. Other countries are also seeing falling rates of discovery and extraction, and world conventional crude oil production has flatlined for the past six years, even as oil prices have soared. According to the International Energy Agency, world conventional crude oil production peaked in 2006 and will taper off from now on.

ExxonMobil says this is nothing we should worry about, as there are still vast untapped hydrocarbon reserves all over the world. That's true. But we have already harvested the low-hanging fruit of our oil and gas endowment. The resources that remain are of lower quality and are located in places that are harder to access than was the case for oil and gas in decades past. Oil and gas companies are increasingly operating in ultra-deep water, or in arctic regions, and need to use sophisticated technologies like hydrofracturing, horizontal drilling, and water or nitrogen injection. We have entered the era of extreme hydrocarbons. This means that production costs will continue to escalate year after year. Even if we get rid of oil market speculators, the price of oil will keep ratcheting up anyway. And we know from recent economic history that soaring energy prices cause the economy to wither: when consumers have to spend much more on gasoline, they have less to spend on everything else.

But if investment costs for oil and gas exploration and extraction are increasing rapidly, the environmental costs of these fuels are ballooning just as quickly. With the industry operating at the limits of its technical know-how, mistakes can and will happen. As we saw in the Gulf of Mexico in the summer of 2010, mistakes that occur under a mile or two of ocean water can have devastating consequences for an entire ecosystem, and for people who depend on that ecosystem. The citizens of the Gulf coast are showing a brave face to the world and understandably want to believe their seafood industry is safe and recovering, but biologists who work there tell us that oil from the Deepwater Horizon disaster is still working its way up the food chain.

Of course the biggest environmental cost from burning fossil fuels comes from our chemical alteration of the planetary atmosphere. Carbon dioxide from oil, gas, and coal combustion is changing Earth's climate and causing our oceans to acidify. The likely consequences are truly horrifying: rising seas, extreme weather, falling agricultural output, and collapsing oceanic food chains. Never mind starving polar bears—we're facing the prospect of starving people.

But wait: Is this even happening? Nearly half of all Americans tell pollsters they think either the planet isn't warming at all, or, if it is, it's not because of fossil fuels. After all, how can the world really be getting hotter when we're seeing record snowfalls in many places? And even if it *is* warming, how do we know that's not because of volcanoes, or natural climate variation, or cow farts, or because the Sun is getting hotter? Americans are understandably confused by questions like these, which they hear repeated again and again on radio and television.

Now of course, if you apply the critical thinking skills you've learned here at WPI to an examination of the relevant data, you'll probably come to the same conclusion as the overwhelming majority of scientists who have studied these questions. Indeed, the scientific community is nearly unanimous in assessing that the Earth *is* warming, and that the only credible explanation for this is rising levels of carbon dioxide from the burning of fossil fuels. That kind of consensus is hard to achieve among scientists except when a conclusion is overwhelmingly supported by evidence.

I'm not out to demonize ExxonMobil, but some things have to be said. That company has played a pivotal role in shaping our national conversation about climate change. A 2007 report from the Union of Concerned Scientists described how ExxonMobil adopted the tobacco industry's disinformation tactics, and funded some of the same organizations that led campaigns against tobacco regulation in the 1980s—but this time to cloud public understanding of climate change science and delay action on the issue. According to the report, between 1998 and 2005 ExxonMobil funneled almost 16 million dollars to a network of 43 advocacy organizations that misrepresented peer-reviewed scientific findings about global warming science. Exxon raised doubts about even the most indisputable scientific evidence, attempted to portray its opposition to action as a positive quest for "sound science" rather than business self-interest, and used its access to the Bush administration to block federal policies and shape government communications on global warming. All of this is well documented.

And it worked. Over the course of the past few years one of our nation's two main political parties has made climate change *denial* a litmus test for its candidates, which means that climate legislation is effectively unachievable in this country for the foreseeable future. This is a big victory for ExxonMobil. Its paltry 16-million-dollar investment will likely translate to many times that amount in unregulated profits. But it is a disaster for democracy, for the Earth, and for your generation.

But here's the thing. Everyone knows that America and the world will have to transition off of fossil fuels during this century anyway. Mr. Tillerson knows it as well as anyone. Some people evidently want to delay that transition as long as possible, but it cannot be put off indefinitely. My colleagues at Post Carbon Institute and I believe that delaying this transition is extremely dangerous for a number of reasons. Obviously, it prolongs the environmental impacts from fossil fuel production and combustion. But also, the process of building a renewable energy economy will take decades and require a tremendous amount of investment. If we don't start soon enough, society will get caught in a trap of skyrocketing fuel prices and a collapsing economy, and won't be in a position to fund needed work on alternative energy development. In my darker moments I fear that we have already waited too long and that it is already too late. I hope I'm not right about that, and when I talk to young people like you I tend to feel that we *can* make this great transition, and that actions that have seemed politically impossible for the past 40 years will become inevitable as circumstances change, and as new hearts and minds come to the table.

Even in the best case, though, the fact that we have waited so long to address our addiction to oil will still present us with tremendous challenges. But this is not a problem for ExxonMobil, at least not anytime soon. When the price of oil goes up, we feel the pain while Exxon reaps the profits. Even though Exxon's actual oil production is falling due to the depletion of its oilfields, corporate revenues are high: Exxon made almost eleven billion dollars in profits in just the past three months. This translates to jobs in the oil industry. But how about the renewable energy industry, which everyone agrees is the key to our future?

For the past 40 years, every US president without exception has said we must reduce our country's dependence on imported petroleum. Addiction to oil has become our nation's single greatest point of geopolitical, economic, and environmental vulnerability. Yet here we are in 2011, still driving a fleet of two hundred million gasoline-guzzling cars, trucks, and SUVs. The inability of our elected officials to tackle such an obvious problem is not simply the result of ineptitude. In addition to funding climate denial, fossil fuel companies like Exxon have contributed to politicians' election campaigns in order to gain perks for their industry and put off higher efficiency standards and environmental protections. Denying looming fuel supply problems, discouraging a transition to renewable energy, distorting climate science—these are all understandable tactics from the standpoint of corporate self-interest. Exxon is just doing what corporations do. But once again, it is society as a whole that suffers, and the consequences will fall especially on your generation.

Mr. Tillerson may have informed you about his company's Global Climate and Energy Project at Stanford University. Exxon is now funding research into lowering the cost and increasing the efficiency of solar photovoltaic devices, increasing the efficiency of fuel cells, increasing the energy capacity of lithium-ion batteries for electric cars, designing higher-efficiency engines that produce lower emissions, making biodiesel fuel from bacteria, and improving carbon capture and storage. This is all admirable, if it is genuine and not just window dressing. Here's a reality check in that regard: Exxon is investing about ten million dollars a year in the Global Climate and Energy Project—an amount that almost exactly equals Mr. Tillerson's personal compensation in 2010. Ten million dollars also equals about three hours' worth of Exxon profits from last year. You tell me if you think that is a sensibly proportionate response to the problems of climate change and oil depletion from the world's largest energy company.

Even if Exxon's investments in a sustainable energy future were of an appropriate scale, they come late in the game. We are still in a bind. That's because there is no magic-bullet energy source out there that will enable world energy supplies to continue to grow as fossil fuels dwindle. Renewable energy is viable and necessary, and we should be doing far more to develop it. But solar, wind, geothermal, tidal, and wave power each have limits and drawbacks that will keep them from supplying energy as cheaply and as abundantly as we would like. Our bind is that we have built our existing transport infrastructure and food systems around energy sources that are becoming more problematic with every passing year, and we have no Plan B in place. This means we will probably have less energy in the future, rather than more.

Again, I am addressing my words especially to you students. This will be the defining reality of your lives. Whatever field you go into—business, finance, engineering, transportation, agriculture, education, or entertainment—your experience will be shaped by the energy transition that is now under way. The better you understand this, the more effectively you will be able to contribute to society and make your way in the world.

We are at one of history's great turning points. During your lifetime you will see world changes more significant in scope than human beings have ever witnessed before. You will have the opportunity to participate in the redesign of the basic systems that support our society—our energy system, food system, transport system, and financial system. I say this with some confidence, because our existing energy, food, transport, and financial systems can't be maintained under the circumstances that are developing—circumstances of fossil fuel depletion and an unstable climate. As a result, what you choose to do in life could have far greater implications than you may currently realize.

Over the course of your lifetime society will need to solve some basic problems:

- How to grow food sustainably without fossil fuel inputs and without eroding topsoil or drawing down increasingly scarce supplies of fresh water;
- How to support seven billion people (and counting) without depleting natural resources—including forests, fish, and finite stocks of minerals and metals; and
- How to reorganize our financial system so that it can continue to perform its essential functions—reinvesting savings into socially beneficial projects—in the context of an economy that is stable or shrinking due to declining energy supplies, rather than continually growing.

Each of these core problems will take time, intelligence, and courage to solve. This is a challenge suitable for heroes and heroines, one that's big enough to keep even the greatest generation in history fully occupied. If every crisis is an opportunity, then this is the biggest opportunity humanity has ever seen.

Making the best of the circumstances that life sends our way is perhaps the most important attitude and skill that we can hope to develop. The circumstance that life is currently serving up is one of fundamentally changed economic conditions. As this decade and this century wear on, average Americans will have fewer material goods and will be less mobile. In a few years we will look back on late 20th-century America as a time and place of advertising-stoked consumption that was completely out of proportion to what Nature can sustainably provide. I suspect we will think of those times—with a combination of longing and regret—as a lost golden age of abundance, but also an era of foolishness and greed that put the entire world at risk.

Making the best of our new circumstances will mean finding happiness in designing higher-quality products that can be reused, repaired, and recycled almost endlessly and finding fulfillment in human relationships and cultural activities rather than mindless shopping. Fortunately, we know from recent cross-cultural psychological studies that there is little correlation between levels of consumption and levels of happiness. That tells us that life can in fact be better without fossil fuels.

So whether we view these as hard times or as times of great possibility is really a matter of perspective. I would emphasize the latter. This is a time of unprecedented opportunity for service to one's community. It's a time when it will be possible to truly change the world, because the world has to change anyway. It is a time when you can make a difference by helping to shape this needed and inevitable change.

As I travel, I meet young people in every part of this country who are taking up the challenge of building a post-petroleum future: a 25-year-old farmer in New Jersey who plows with horses and uses no chemicals; the operator of a biodiesel co-op in Northampton, Massachusetts; a solar installer in Oakland, California. The energy transition will require new thinking in every field you can imagine, from fine arts to banking. Companies everywhere are hiring sustainability officers to help guide them through the challenges and opportunities. At the same time, many young people are joining energy and climate activist initiatives like 350.org and the Transition movement.

So here is my message to you in a nutshell. Fossil fuels made it possible to build the world you lived in as a child and later as a student all through your school years. Now it's up to you to imagine and build the world after fossil fuels. This is the challenge and opportunity of your lifetimes. I wish you good cheer and good luck as you make the most of it.

— MAY 2011

9

▶ THE FIGHT OF THE CENTURY

A S THE WORLD ECONOMY CRASHES AGAINST DEBT AND RE-source limits, many countries are responding by attempting to salvage what are actually their most expendable features—corrupt, insolvent banks and bloated militaries—while leaving the majority of their people to languish in "austerity." This has resulted in a series of uprisings, taking a variety of forms in different nations. Such conditions and responses will lead, sooner or later, to social as well as economic upheaval—and a collapse of the support infrastructure on which billions depend for their very survival.

Nations could, in principle, forestall social collapse by providing the bare essentials of existence (food, water, housing, medical care, family planning, education, employment for those able to work, and public safety) universally and in a way that could be sustained for some time, while paying for this by deliberately shrinking other features of society—starting with military and financial sectors—and by taxing the wealthy. The cost of covering the basics for everyone is still within the means of most nations. Providing human necessities would not remove all the fundamental problems now converging (climate change, resource depletion, and the need for fundamental economic reforms), but it would provide a platform of social stability and equity to give the world time to grapple with deeper, existential challenges.

Unfortunately, many governments are averse to this course of action. And if they did provide universal safety nets, ongoing economic contraction might still result in conflict, though in this instance it might arise from groups opposed to the perceived failures of "big government."

Further, even in the best instance, safety nets can only buy time. The capacity of governments to maintain flows of money and goods will erode. Thus it will increasingly be up to households and communities to provide the basics for themselves while reducing their dependence upon, and vulnerability to, centralized systems of financial and governmental power.

This will set up a fundamental contradiction. *When the government tries to provide people the basics, power is centralized—but as the capacity of the government wanes, it can feel threatened by people trying to provide the basics for themselves and act to discourage or even criminalize them.*

Theorists on both the far left and far right of the political spectrum have advocated for the decentralization of food, finance, education, and other basic societal support systems for decades. Some efforts toward decentralization (such as the local food movement) have led to the development of niche markets. However, here we are talking about not just the incremental growth of social movements or marginal industries, but what may become the signal economic and social trend for the remainder of the 21st century—a trend that is currently ignored and resisted by governmental, economic, and media elites who can't imagine an alternative beyond the dichotomies of free enterprise versus planned economy, or Keynesian stimulus versus austerity.

The decentralized provision of basic necessities is not likely to flow from a utopian vision of a perfect or even improved society (as have some social movements of the past). It will emerge instead from iterative human responses to a daunting and worsening set of environmental and economic problems, and it will in many instances be impeded and opposed by politicians, bankers, and industrialists.

It is this contest between traditional power elites and growing masses of disenfranchised poor and formerly middle-class people attempting to provide the necessities of life for themselves in the context of a shrinking economy that is shaping up to be the fight of the century.

When Civilizations Decline

In his benchmark 1988 book *The Collapse of Complex Societies*,[1] archaeologist Joseph Tainter explained the rise and demise of civilizations in terms of complexity. He used the word *complexity* to refer to "the size of a society, the number and distinctiveness of its parts, the variety of specialized social roles that it incorporates, the number of distinct social personalities present, and the variety of mechanisms for organizing these into a coherent, functioning whole."[2]

Civilizations are complex societies organized around cities; they obtain their food from agriculture (field crops), use writing and mathematics, and maintain full-time division of labor. They are centralized, with people and resources constantly flowing from the hinterlands toward urban hubs. Thousands of cultures have flourished throughout the human past, but there have only been about 24 civilizations. And all—except our current global industrial civilization (so far)—have ultimately collapsed.

Tainter describes the growth of civilization as a process of investing societal resources in the development of ever-greater complexity in order to solve problems. For example, in village-based tribal societies an arms race between tribes can erupt, requiring each village to become more centralized and complexly organized in order to fend off attacks. But complexity costs energy. As Tainter puts it, "More complex societies are costlier to maintain than simpler ones and require higher support levels per capita." Since available energy and resources are limited, a point therefore comes when increasing investments become too costly and yield declining marginal returns. Even the maintenance of existing levels of complexity costs too much (citizens may experience this as onerous levels of taxation), and a general simplification and decentralization of society ensues—a process colloquially referred to as *collapse*.

During such times societies typically see sharply declining population levels, and the survivors experience severe hardship. Elites lose their grip on power. Domestic revolutions and foreign wars erupt. People flee cities and establish new, smaller communities in the hinterlands. Governments fall and new sets of power relations emerge.

It is frightening to think about what collapse would mean for our current global civilization. Nevertheless, as we are about to see, there are good reasons for concluding that our civilization is reaching the limits of centralization and complexity, that marginal returns on investments in complexity are declining, and that simplification and decentralization are inevitable.

Thinking in terms of simplification, contraction, and decentralization is more accurate and helpful, and probably less scary, than contemplating collapse. It also opens avenues for foreseeing, reshaping, and even harnessing inevitable social processes so as to minimize hardship and maximize possible benefits.

Why Contraction, Simplification, and Decentralization Are Inevitable

The premise that a simplification of global industrial civilization is soon inevitable is the summarized conclusion of a robust discourse developed in scores of books and hundreds of scientific papers during the past four decades, drawing upon developments in the studies of ecology, the history of civilizations, the economics of energy, and systems theory. This premise can be stated as follows:

- The dramatic increase in societal complexity seen during the past two centuries (measured, for example, in a relentless trend toward urbanization and soaring volumes of trade) resulted primarily from increasing rates of energy flow for manufacturing and transport. Fossil fuels provided by far the biggest energy subsidy in human history, and were responsible for industrialization, urbanization, and massive population growth.
- Today, as conventional fossil fuels rapidly deplete, world energy flows appear set to decline. While there are enormous amounts

of unconventional fossil fuels yet to be exploited, these will soon be so costly to extract—in monetary, energy, and environmental terms—that continued growth in *available* fossil energy supplies is unlikely; meanwhile alternative energy sources remain largely undeveloped and will require extraordinary levels of investment if they are to make up for declines in fossil energy.

- Declining rates of energy flow and declining energy quality will have predictable direct effects: higher real energy prices, the need for increased energy efficiency in all sectors of society, and an ever-greater proportion of increasingly scarce investment capital being directed toward the energy sector.

- Some of the effects of declining energy will be nonlinear and unpredictable, and could lead to a general collapse of civilization. Economic contraction will not be as gradual and orderly as economic expansion has been. Such effects may include an uncontrollable and catastrophic unwinding of the global system of credit, finance, and trade, or the dramatic expansion of warfare as a result of heightened competition for energy resources or the protection of trade privileges.

- Large-scale trade requires money, and so economic growth has required an ongoing expansion of currency, credit, and debt. It is possible, however, for credit and debt to expand *faster* than the energy-fed "real" economy of manufacturing and trade; when this happens, the result is a credit/debt bubble, which must eventually deflate—usually resulting in massive destruction of capital and extreme economic distress. During the past few decades, the industrialized world has inflated the largest credit/debt bubble in human history.

- As resource consumption has burgeoned during the past century, so have its environmental impacts. Droughts and floods are becoming more frequent and intense, straining food systems while also imposing direct monetary costs (many of which are ultimately borne by the insurance industry). These impacts—primarily arising from global climate change driven by our consumption of fossil fuels—now threaten to undermine not only economic growth, but also the ecological basis of civilization.

To summarize this already brief summary: Due to energy limits, overwhelming debt burdens, and accumulating environmental impacts, the world has reached a point where continued economic growth may be unachievable. Instead of increasing its complexity, therefore, society will—for the foreseeable future, and probably in fits and starts—be shedding complexity.

General economic contraction has arguably already begun in Europe and the United States. The signs are everywhere. High unemployment levels, stagnating or declining energy consumption, and jittery markets herald what some bearish financial analysts describe as a "greater depression" perhaps lasting until midcentury.[3] But even that stark assessment misses the true dimensions of the crisis because it focuses only on its financial and social manifestations while ignoring its energy and ecological basis.

Whether or not the root causes of worldwide economic turmoil are generally understood, that turmoil is already impacting political systems as well as the daily lives of hundreds of millions of people. Governments and central banks anxious to avert a contagious deflationary destruction of global capital have bailed out banks that innovated their way into insolvency in the years leading up to 2008. Meanwhile, governments that borrowed heavily during the last decade or two with the expectation that further economic growth would swell tax revenues and make it easy to repay debts now find real growth hard to achieve.

In a few instances, the very financial institutions that some governments temporarily saved from insolvency are now undermining the economies of other governments by forcing a downgrade of their credit ratings, making debt rollovers more difficult. Those latter governments are being given an ultimatum: reduce domestic spending or face exclusion from the system of global capital. But in many cases government spending is all that's keeping the national economy functioning. Increasingly, even in countries recently considered good credit risks, the costs of preventing a collapse of the financial sector are being shifted to the general populace by way of austerity measures that result in economic contraction and general misery.

A global popular uprising is the predictable result of governments' cuts in social services, their efforts to shield wealthy investors from consequences of their own greed, and rising food and fuel prices. In recent years, recurring protests have erupted in Africa, the Middle East, Asia, Europe, and North America. The long-range aims of protesters are in many cases unformulated or unarticulated, but the immediate reasons for the protests are not hard to discern. As food and fuel prices squeeze, poor people naturally feel the pinch first. When the poor are still able to get by, they are often reluctant to risk assembling in the street to oppose corrupt, entrenched regimes. When they can no longer make ends meet, the risks of protest seem less significant— there is nothing to lose; life is intolerable anyway. Widespread protest opens the opportunity for needed political and economic reforms, but it also leads to the prospect of bloody crackdowns and reduced social and political stability.

Scenarios for Societal Simplification

If the above premise is correct, then two scenarios can easily be envisioned:

A. Continued (ever-more desperate) pursuit of business-as-usual. In this scenario, policy makers try restarting economic growth with stimulus spending and bailouts; all efforts are directed toward increasing, or at least maintaining, the complexity and centralization of society. Deficits are disregarded.

This was the general strategy for many governments in recent years as they grappled with the first phase of the global financial crisis. The US and stronger members of the EU experienced tangible but limited success at engineering a recovery and averting a deflationary meltdown of their economies through deficit spending. However, the fundamental problems that led to the 2008 crisis were merely papered over.

The limits of this course of action have been revealing themselves as the US "recovery" fails to gain much traction, Chinese growth winds down, and the European Union slips in and out of recession. Further stimulus spending would require another massive round of government borrowing, and that would face strong domestic political headwinds as well as resistance from the financial community (in the form of credit downgrades, which would make further borrowing more expensive).

Meanwhile, despite much talk about the potential for low-grade unconventional sources of oil such as tar sands and tight oil, world energy supplies are in essentially the same straits as they were at the start of the 2008 crisis (which, it is important to recall, was partly triggered by a historic oil price spike). And without increasing and affordable energy flows a genuine economic recovery (meaning a return to growth in manufacturing and trade) may not be possible. Thus financial pump priming will yield diminishing returns.

The pursuit of business-as-usual appears merely to lead us back to the sort of turmoil seen in 2008; however, next time the situation will be worse, as governments and central banks will already have exhausted most of the economic stimulus ammunition. If they are able to get ahead of debt deflation and deleveraging by the massive "printing" of new money, the eventual result will be hyperinflation and currency collapse.

B. Simplification by austerity. In this scenario, nations pull back from their current state of overindebtedness and placate bond markets by cutting domestic social spending and withdrawing safety nets put in place during the past few decades of steady growth. This strategy is being adopted by the United States and many EU nations, partly out of perceived necessity and partly on the advice of economists who promise that domestic social spending cuts (along with privatization of government services) will spur more private-sector economic activity and thereby lead to a sustainable recovery.

The evidence for the efficacy of austerity as a path to increased economic health is spotty at best in "normal" economic times. Under current circumstances, there is overwhelming evidence that it leads to declining economic performance as well as social unraveling. In nations where the austerity prescription has been most vigorously applied (Ireland, Greece, Spain, Italy, and Portugal), contraction has continued or even accelerated, and popular protest is on the rise. Even Germany, Europe's strongest economy, is being impacted. As Jeff Madrick has argued in the *New York Review of Books*,[4] policy makers are failing to see that rising deficits are more a *symptom* of slower economic growth than the *cause*.

Austerity is having similar effects in states, counties, and cities in the United States. State and local governments cut roughly half a million jobs during 2009–10; had they kept hiring at their previous pace to keep up with population growth, they would instead have added a half-million jobs. Meanwhile, due to low tax revenues, local governments are allowing paved roads to turn to gravel, closing libraries and parks, and laying off public employees.

It's not hard to recognize a self-reinforcing feedback loop at work here. A shrinking economy means declining tax revenues, which make it harder for governments to repay debt. In order to avoid a credit downgrade, governments must cut spending. This shrinks the economy further, eventually resulting in credit downgrades anyway. That in turn raises the cost of borrowing. So government must cut spending even further to remain credit-worthy. The *need* for social spending explodes as unemployment, homelessness, and malnutrition increase, while the *availability* of social services declines. The only apparent way out of this death spiral is a revival of rapid economic growth. But if the premise above is correct, that is a mere pipedream.

Both of these scenarios lead to unacceptable and unstable outcomes. Aren't there other possibilities? Well, yes. Here are two.

C. Centralized provision of the basics. In this scenario, nations directly provide jobs and basic necessities to the general public while deliberately simplifying, downsizing, or eliminating expendable features of society such as the financial sector and the military, and taxing those who can afford it—wealthy individuals, banks, and larger businesses— at higher rates. This is the path outlined at the start of the essay; at this point it is appropriate to add a bit more detail.

In many cases, centralized provision of basic necessities is relatively cheap and efficient. For example, since the beginning of the current financial crisis the US government has mainly gone about creating jobs by channeling tax breaks and stimulus spending to the private sector. But this has turned out to be an extremely costly and inefficient way of providing jobs, far more of which could be called into existence (per dollar spent) by direct government hiring.[5] Similarly, the new US federal policy of increasing the public's access to health care by requiring individuals to purchase private medical insurance is more costly than simply providing a universal government-run health insurance program, as every other industrial nation does. If Britain's experience during and immediately after World War II is any guide, then better access to higher-quality food could be ensured with a government-run rationing program than through a fully privatized food system. And government banks could arguably provide a more reliable public service than private banks, which funnel enormous streams of unearned income to bankers and investors. If all this sounds like an argument for utopian socialism, read on—it's not. But there are indeed real benefits to be reaped from government provision of necessities, and it would be foolish to ignore them.

A parallel line of reasoning goes like this. Immediately after natural disasters or huge industrial accidents, the people impacted typically turn to the state for aid. As the global climate chaotically changes, and as the hunt for ever-lower-grade fossil energy sources forces companies to drill deeper and in more sensitive areas, we will undoubtedly see worsening weather crises, environmental degradation and pollution, and industrial accidents such as oil spills. Inevitably, more and more families and communities will be relying upon state-provided aid for disaster relief.[6]

Many people would be tempted to view an expansion of state support services with alarm as the ballooning of the powers of an already bloated central government. There may well be substance to this fear, depending on how the strategy is pursued. But it is important to remember that the economy as a whole, in this scenario, would be contracting—and would continue to contract—due to resource limits. Think of state provision of services not as utopian socialism (whether that phrase is viewed positively or negatively) but as a strategic reorganization of society in pursuit of greater efficiency in times of scarcity. Perhaps the best analogy would be with wartime rationing, a practice in which government takes on a larger role in managing distribution so as to free up resources for fighting a common enemy.

How to pay for such an expansion of services in a time of overindebtedness and scarce credit? The financial industry could be downsized by taxing financial transactions and unearned income. Further, the national government could create its own financing directly, without having to borrow from banks. One might think that if government can just create as much money as it wants, then it could do away with scarcity altogether. But in the end it's not money that makes the world go 'round. With energy and resources in short supply, the real economy would continue to shrink no matter how much money the central government printed; overprinting would simply result in hyperinflation. However, up to a point, efficiency gains and equitable distribution could minimize human misery even as the economic pie continued to shrink.

Some nations have already begun to make policy shifts along the lines suggested in this scenario: Ecuador, for example, has expanded direct public employment, enforced social security provisions for all workers, diversified its economy to reduce dependence on oil exports, and enlarged public banking operations.[7]

In some large industrial nations, such as the United States, entrenched interests (principally, the fossil-fuel, financial, and weapons industries) would work to prevent movement in these directions—as they are already doing. Meanwhile, the fact that the economy was still contracting even in the face of strenuous government efforts might lead many people to believe that contraction was occurring *because of* government, and so popular opposition to government (from some quarters at least) might increase. Government might be motivated to crush such dissent in order to maintain stability (this, of course, is what far-right antigovernment groups most fear). A nation that remained stuck in option C for decades would likely come to resemble the Soviet Union or Cuba. It might also resort to extreme efforts to stoke patriotic sentiment as a way of justifying repression of dissent.

In any case, it's hard to say how long this strategy could be maintained in the face of declining energy supplies. Eventually, central authorities' ability to operate and repair the infrastructure necessary to continue supporting the general citizenry might erode to the point that the center would no longer hold. At that stage, Strategy C would fade out and Strategy D would fade in.

D. Local provision of the basics. Suppose that, as economies contract, national governments fail to step up to provide the basics of existence to their citizens. Or (as just discussed) suppose those efforts wane over time due to an inability to maintain national-scale infrastructure. In this final scenario, local governments, ad hoc social movements, and nongovernmental organizations could organize the provision of basic necessities. These groups could include small businesses, churches and cults, street gangs with an expanded mission, and formal or informal cooperative enterprises of all sorts.

In the absence of global transport networks, electricity grids, and other elements of infrastructure that bind modern nations together, whatever levels of support that can originate locally would provide a mere shadow of the standard of living currently enjoyed by middle-class Americans or Europeans. Just one telling example: we will likely never see families getting together in church basements to manufacture laptop computers or cell phones from scratch. The ongoing local provision of food and the simplest of manufactured goods is a reasonable possibility, given intelligent, cooperative effort; for the most part, however, during the next few decades a truly local economy will be mostly a salvage economy.[8]

If central governments seek to maintain complexity at the expense of more dispersed governmental nodes (city, county, and state governments), then conflict between communities and sputtering national or global power hubs is likely. Communities may begin to withdraw streams of support from central authorities—and not only governmental authorities, but financial and corporate ones as well.

In recent decades, communities have seen it as being in their interest to give national and global corporations tax breaks and other subsidies for locating factories and stores within the local tax-shed. Analysis after-the-fact is showing that in many instances this was a poor bargain: tax revenues have been insufficient to make up for new infrastructure costs (roads, sewer, water); meanwhile, most of the wealth generated by factories and mega-store outlets tends to find its way to distant corporate headquarters and Wall Street investors.[9] Increasingly, communities are recognizing big chain retail corporations (and big banks as well) as parasites siphoning away local capital, and are looking for ways to support small, local businesses and banks instead.

City and county governments are just beginning to adopt a similar attitude toward federal and state governments. Formerly, larger governmental entities provided subsidies for local infrastructure projects and antipoverty programs. As funding streams for those projects and programs dry up, local governments find themselves increasingly in competition with their cash-starved big brothers.

If communities have to contend with declining tax revenues, competition from larger governments, and predatory mega-corporations and banks, then nonprofit organizations—which support tens of thousands of local charity efforts—face perhaps even greater challenges. The current philanthropic model rests entirely upon assumed economic growth: foundation grants come from returns on the foundation's investments (in the stock market and elsewhere). As economic growth slows and reverses, the world of nonprofit organizations will shake and crumble, and the casualties will include tens of thousands of social services agencies, educational programs, and environmental protection organizations…as well as countless symphony orchestras, dance ensembles, museums, and on and on.

If national government loses its grip, if local governments are pinched simultaneously from above and below, and if nonprofit organizations are starved for funding, from where will come the means to support local communities with the social and cultural services they need? Local businesses and co-ops (including cooperative banks, otherwise known as credit unions) could shoulder some of the burden if they are able to remain profitable and avoid falling victim to big banks and mega-corporations before the latter go under.

The next line of support would come from the volunteer efforts of people willing to work hard for the common good. Every town and city is replete with churches and service organizations. Many of these would be well placed to help educate and organize the general populace to facilitate survival and recovery—especially some of the more recent arrivals, such as the Transition Initiatives, which already have collapse preparedness as a raison d'être. In the best instance, volunteer efforts would get under way well before crisis hits, organizing farmers' markets, ride- and car-share programs, local currencies, and "buy local" campaigns. There is a growing body of literature intended to help that pre-crisis effort; a recent worthy entry in that field is *Local Dollars, Local Sense: How to Shift Your Money from Wall Street to Main Street and Achieve Real Prosperity*, by Michael Shuman.[10]

The final source of support would consist of families and neighborhoods banding together to do whatever is necessary to survive—grow gardens, keep chickens, reuse, repurpose, repair, defend, share, and, if all else fails, learn to do without. People would move into shared housing to cut costs. They would look out for one another to maintain safety and security. These extreme-local practices would sometimes fly against the headwinds of local and national regulations. In those cases, even if they're in no place to help materially, local governments could lend a hand simply by getting out of the way—for example, by changing zoning ordinances to allow new uses of space. (Or in more urgent situations, they might use land banks and eminent domain to take over unused real estate and make it available for community purposes.[11]) Thus enabled, neighborhood committees could identify vacant houses and commercial spaces and turn these into community gardens and meeting centers. In return, as neighborhoods network with other neighborhoods, a stronger social fabric might reinvigorate local government.

As discussed above, movements to support localization—however benign their motives—may be perceived by national authorities as a threat. Where national governments see local citizens' demands for greater autonomy as menacing, the response could include surveillance, denial of right to public assembly, infiltration of protest organizations, militarization of the police, the development of an increasing array of nonlethal weapons for use against protesters, the adoption of laws that abrogate the rights to trial and evidentiary hearings—and in extreme cases, torture and the deployment of death squads. Canadian activist Leah Henderson, in a letter written to fellow dissidents prior to being sent to prison for her role in the 2010 G20 summit protests, observed tellingly that, "My skills and experience—as a facilitator, as a trainer, as a legal professional and as someone linking different communities and movements—were all targeted in this case, with the state trying to depict me as a 'brainwasher' and as a mastermind of mayhem, violence and destruction.... It is clear that the skills that make us strong, *the alternatives that reduce our reliance on their systems* [emphasis added] and prefigure a new world, are the very things that they are most afraid of."[12]

Altogether, the road to localism may not be as easy and cheerful a path as some proponents portray. It will be filled with hard work, pitfalls, conflicts, and struggle—as well as comradeship, community, and comity. Its ultimate advantage: the primary trends of the current century (discussed above) seem to lead ultimately in this direction. If all else fails, the local matrix of neighbors, family, and friends will offer our last refuge.

Complications

Scenarios are not forecasts; they are planning tools. As prophecies, they're not much more reliable than dreams. What really happens in the years ahead will be shaped as much by "black swan" events as by trends in resource depletion or credit markets. We know that environmental impacts from climate change will intensify, but we don't know exactly where, when, or how severely those impacts will manifest; meanwhile, there is always the possibility of a massive environmental disaster not caused by human activity (such as an earthquake or volcanic eruption) occurring in such a location or on such a scale as to substantially alter the course of world events. Wars are also impossible to predict in terms of intensity and outcome, yet we know that geopolitical tensions are building. It is just possible (not very, but just) that some new energy technology—such as cold fusion—could reset the collapse clock, enabling the global economy to lurch along for another couple of decades before humanity breaches the next crucial natural limit. The simplification of society is likely to be a complicated and surprising process. Nevertheless, the four scenarios offered here do provide a rudimentary map of some of the main possibilities for societal response.

These scenarios are not mutually exclusive. A single nation might traverse two, three, or all of them over a period of years or decades.

If our premise is correct, then Strategy A (the pursuit of business-as-usual) is inherently untenable except over the very short term; it must soon give way to B, C, or D.

Strategy B (austerity) seems to lead, via social and economic disintegration, quickly to D (local provision of the basics), as evidenced in a 2012 *New York Times* article about Greeks reverting to subsistence farming in the face of government cutbacks.[13]

Strategy C (central provision of the basics) would probably lead to D as well, though the path would likely take longer—possibly much longer—to traverse. In other words, all roads appear to lead eventually to localism; the questions are: how and when shall we arrive there, and in what condition? (And, how local?)

The route via austerity has the virtue of being quicker, but only because it induces more misery more suddenly.

Centralized provision of essentials might be merely a way of prolonging the agony of collapse—unless authorities understand the inevitable trend of events and deliberately plan for a gradual shift from central to local provision of basic needs. The US could do this by, for example, enacting agricultural policies to favor small commercial farms and subsistence farms while removing subsidies from big agribusiness. Outsourcing, offshoring, and other practices that serve the interests of global capital at the expense of local communities could be discouraged through regulation and taxation, while domestic manufacturers could be favored (this "protectionism" would no doubt be decried both domestically and internationally). Altogether, the *planned* transition from C to D may constitute its own scenario, perhaps the best of the lot in its likely outcomes.

The success of governments in navigating the transitions ahead may depend on measurable qualities and characteristics of governance itself. In this regard, there could be useful clues to be gleaned from the World Governance Index,[14] which assesses governments according to criteria of peace and security, rule of law, human rights and participation, sustainable development, and human development. For 2011, the United States ranked number 32 (and falling: it was number 28 in 2008)—behind Uruguay, Estonia, and Portugal but ahead of China (number 140) and Russia (number 148).

On the other hand, "collapse preparedness" (Dmitry Orlov's memorable phrase) may coexist with governmental practices that appear inefficient and even repressive in pre-collapse conditions. In his book *Reinventing Collapse*,[15] Orlov makes the case that the Soviet Union, for all its dreariness and poor governance, provided more collapse preparedness than does the United States today, partly because people's expectations in the USSR were already low after decades spent barely getting by. Or was the USSR's high level of collapse preparedness largely a matter of its having long guaranteed the very basics of existence to its people? No one became homeless when the Soviet system disintegrated, since no one had a mortgage to be foreclosed upon; when the economy crashed, people simply stayed where they were.

In the era of economic contraction governmental competence will not determine all the prospects of nations. Demographics will also be decisive: Egypt's political and social tumult has been driven not just by weariness with corruption, but also by high birth rates—which have led to 83 percent unemployment for those between 15 and 29, inadequate education, high poverty rates, and a growing inability of the nation to feed itself (about half of Egypt's food is now imported). Perhaps it could be argued that one of the first signs of competent governance is effective population policy.

For the sake of any national policy maker who may be reading this essay, here are a few take-home bullet points that summarize most of the advice that can be gleaned from our scenario exercise:

- Guarantee the basics of existence to the general public for as long as possible.
- At the same time, promote local production of essential goods, strengthen local social interconnectivity, and shore up local economies.
- Promote environmental protection and resource conservation, reducing reliance on fossil fuels in every way possible.
- Stabilize population levels.
- Foster sound governance (especially in terms of participation and transparency).
- Provide universal education in practical skills (gardening, cooking, bicycle repair, sewing, etc.) as well as in basic academic subjects (reading, math, science, critical thinking, and history). And finally,
- Don't be evil—that is, don't succumb to the temptation to deploy military tactics against your own people as you feel your grip on power slipping; the process of decentralization is inexorable, so plan to facilitate it.

One wonders how many big-government centralists of the left, right, or center—who often see the stability of the state, the status of their own careers, and the ultimate good of the people as being virtually identical—are likely to embrace such a prescription.

Final Thoughts

To reiterate the theme of this essay one last time: The decline in resources available to support societal complexity will generate a centrifugal force that will break up existing economic and governmental power structures everywhere. As a result there is a fight brewing—a protracted and intense one, impacting most if not all countries—over access to a shrinking economic pie. It will manifest not only as competition *among* nations but also as conflicts *within* nations, between power elites and the increasingly impoverished masses.

History teaches us at least as much as scenario exercises can. The convergence of debt bubbles, economic contraction, and extreme inequality is hardly unique to our historical moment. A particularly instructive and fateful previous instance occurred in France in the late 18th century. The result then was the French Revolution, which rid the common people of the burden of supporting an arrogant, entrenched aristocracy, while giving birth to ideals of liberty, equality, and universal brotherhood. However, the revolution also brought with it war, despotism, mass executions—and an utter failure to address underlying economic problems.[16] So often, as happened then, nations suffering under economic contraction double down on militarism rather than downsizing their armies so as to free up resources. They go to war, hoping thereby both to win spoils and to give mobs of angry young men a target for their frustrations other than their own government. The gambit seldom succeeds; Napoleon made it work for a while, but not long. France and (most of) its people did survive the tumult. But then, at the dawn of the 19th century, Europe was on the cusp of another revolution—the fossil-fueled Industrial Revolution—and decades of economic growth shimmered on the horizon. Today we are just starting our long slide down the decline side of the fossil fuel supply curve. Will we handle the inevitable social conflicts more wisely than the French did? Will we learn from history?

Sometimes historic social conflict has taken the form of right-wing groups fighting to oppose and overthrow left-democratic national governments (Germany in the 1920s), sometimes as leftist groups battling center-right or far-right governments (Nicaragua in the 1960s and '70s). There is plenty of potential for both brands of conflict within today's countries, which vary greatly in terms of their likely trajectories. (If you're a mobile global citizen who has the luxury of choosing a country of residence, perhaps this essay can help in assessing your prospects.)

Thinking in big-picture terms is useful for those who have access to information and time for reflection; it provides a sense of perspective and a potential for more effective action. For those of us who sit, Arjuna-like, before the battlefield of the 21st century, the question presents itself: What is our appropriate role? Shall we engage in conflict? Or would it be better to prevent, resolve, or avoid it? Differing circumstances and personal temperaments will lead to differing answers. If this essay were a polemic, it might incite readers to resist and oppose those wielding centralized political and economic power. But that is not my purpose here; rather, it is merely to survey the landscape of conflict so as to see where the points of leverage may lie. It is up to readers to do with this very rudimentary analysis what they will.

If the premise and scenarios outlined above are even vaguely accurate, then localism will sooner or later be our fate and our strategy for survival. It seems fairly clear that, whatever our stance regarding conflict, efforts spent now to learn practical skills, become more self-reliant, and form bonds of trust with neighbors will pay off in the long run.

— FEBRUARY 2012

10

▶ THE ANTHROPOCENE: IT'S **NOT** ALL ABOUT US

TIME TO CELEBRATE! WOO-HOO! IT'S OFFICIAL: WE HUMANS have started a new geological epoch—the *Anthropocene*. Who'd have thought that just one species among millions might be capable of such an amazing accomplishment?

Let's wait to stock up on party favors, though. After all, the Anthropocene could be rather bleak. The reason our epoch has acquired a new name is that future geologists will be able to spot a fundamental discontinuity in the rock strata that document our little slice of time in Earth's multi-billion-year pageant. This discontinuity will be traceable to the results of human presence. Think climate change, ocean acidification, and mass extinction.

Welcome to the Anthropocene: a world that may feature little in the way of multicellular ocean life other than jellyfish, and one whose continents might be dominated by a few generalist species able to quickly occupy new and temporary niches as habitats degrade (rats, crows, and cockroaches come to mind). We humans have started the Anthropocene, and we've proudly named it for ourselves, yet ironically we may not be around to enjoy much of it. The chain of impacts we have initiated could potentially last millions of years, but it's a toss-up whether there will be surviving human geologists to track and comment on it.

To be sure, there are celebrants of the Anthropocene who believe we're just getting started, and that humans can and will shape this new epoch deliberately, intelligently, and durably. Mark Lynas, author of *The God Species*, contends the Anthropocene will require us to think and act differently, but that population, consumption, and the economy can continue to grow despite changes to the Earth system.[1] Stewart Brand says we may no longer have a choice as to whether to utterly remake the natural world; in his words, "We only have a choice of terraforming well. That's the green project for this century."[2] In their book *Love Your Monsters: Postenvironmentalism and the Anthropocene*, Michael Schellenberger and Ted Nordhaus of the Breakthrough Institute say we can create a world where ten billion humans achieve a standard of living allowing them to pursue their dreams, though this will only be possible if we embrace growth, modernization, and technological innovation.[3] Similarly, Emma Marris (who admits to having spent almost no time in wilderness), argues in *Rambunctious Garden: Saving Nature in a Post-Wild World* that wilderness is gone forever, that we should all get used to the idea of the environment as human-constructed, and that this is potentially a good thing.[4]

Is the Anthropocene the culmination of human folly or the commencement of human godhood? Will the emerging epoch be depleted and post-apocalyptic or tastefully appointed by generations of tech-savvy ecosystem engineers? Environmental philosophers are currently engaged in what amounts to a heated debate about the limits of human agency. That discussion is especially engrossing because... *it's all about us!*

The viability of the "we're-in-charge-and-loving-it" version of the Anthropocene—let's call it the *Techno-Anthropocene*—probably hinges on prospects for nuclear power. A concentrated, reliable energy source will be required if we are to maintain and grow industrial civilization, and just about everybody agrees that—whether or not we're at the point of "peak oil"[5]—fossil fuels won't continue energizing civilization for centuries to come. Solar and wind are more environmentally benign sources, but they are diffuse and intermittent. Of society's current non-fossil energy sources, only nuclear is concentrated, available on demand, and (arguably) capable of significant expansion. Thus it's no accident that Techno-Anthropocene boosters such as Mark Lynas, Stewart Brand, Ted Nordhaus, and Michael Schellenberger are also big nuclear proponents.

But the prospects for current nuclear technology are not rosy. The devastating Fukushima meltdowns of 2011 scared off citizens and governments around the globe.[6] Japan will be dealing with the radiation and health impacts for decades if not centuries.[7] There is still no good solution for storing the radioactive waste produced even when reactors are operating as planned.[8] Nuclear power plants are expensive to build and typically suffer from hefty cost over-runs.[9] The world supply of uranium is limited, and shortages are likely by mid-century even with no major expansion of power plants.[10] And, atomic power plants are tied to nuclear weapons proliferation.[11]

In 2012, *The Economist* magazine devoted a special issue to a report on nuclear energy; tellingly, the report was titled, "Nuclear Power: The Dream That Failed."[12] Its conclusion: the nuclear industry may be on the verge of expansion in just a few nations, principally China; elsewhere, it's on life support.[13]

None of this daunts Techno-Anthropocene proponents, who say new nuclear technology has the potential to fulfill the promises originally made for the current fleet of atomic power plants. The centerpiece of this new technology is the integral fast reactor (IFR).

Unlike light water reactors (which comprise the vast majority of nuclear power plants in service today), IFRs would use sodium as a coolant. The IFR nuclear reaction features fast neutrons, and it more thoroughly consumes radioactive fuel, leaving less waste. Indeed, IFRs could use current radioactive waste as fuel. Also, they are alleged to offer greater operational safety and less risk of weapons proliferation.

These arguments are forcefully made in the 2013 documentary "Pandora's Promise," produced and directed by Robert Stone.[14] The film asserts that IFRs are our best tool to mitigate anthropogenic global warming, and goes on to suggest that misguided bureaucrats have deliberately attempted to sabotage the development of IFR reactors.

However, critics of the film say these claims are overblown and that fast-reactor technology is highly problematic. Earlier versions of the fast breeder reactor (of which IFR is a version) were commercial failures and safety disasters. Proponents of the integral fast reactor, say the critics, overlook its exorbitant development and deployment costs and continued proliferation risks. IFR theoretically only "transmutes," rather than eliminates, radioactive waste. Yet the technology is decades away from widespread implementation, and its use of liquid sodium as a coolant can lead to fires and explosions.[15]

David Biello, writing in *Scientific American*, concludes that, "To date, fast neutron reactors have consumed six decades and $100 billion of global effort but remain 'wishful thinking.'"[16]

Even if advocates of IFR reactors are correct, there is one giant practical reason they may not power the Anthropocene: we likely won't see the benefit from them soon enough to make much of a difference. The challenges of climate change and fossil fuel depletion require action now, not decades hence.

Assuming adequate investment capital, and assuming we had decades in which to improve existing technologies, IFR reactors might indeed show significant advantages over current light water reactors (only many years of experience can tell for sure). But we don't have the luxury of limitless investment capital, and we don't have decades in which to work out the bugs and build out this complex, unproven technology.

The Economist's verdict stands: "[N]uclear power will continue to be a creature of politics not economics, with any growth a function of political will or a side-effect of protecting electrical utilities from open competition.... Nuclear power will not go away, but its role may never be more than marginal."

Defying risk of redundancy, I will hammer home the point: cheap, abundant energy is the prerequisite for the Techno-Anthropocene. We can only deal with the challenges of resource depletion and over-population by employing more energy. Running out of fresh water? Just build desalination plants (that use lots of energy). Degrading top-soil in order to produce enough grain to feed ten billion people? Just build millions of hydroponic greenhouses (that need lots of energy for their construction and operation). As we mine deeper deposits of metals and minerals and refine lower-grade ores, we'll require more energy. Energy efficiency gains may help us do more with each increment of power, but a growing population and rising per-capita consumption rates will more than overcome those gains (as they have consistently done in recent decades). Any way you look at it, if we are to maintain industrial society's current growth trajectory we will need more energy, we will need it soon, and our energy sources will have to meet certain criteria—for example, they will need to emit no carbon while at the same time being economically viable.

These essential criteria can be boiled down to four words: *quantity, quality, price,* and *timing*. Nuclear fusion could theoretically provide energy in large amounts, but not soon. The same is true of cold fusion (even if—and it's a big *if*—the process can be confirmed to actually work and can be scaled up). Biofuels offer a very low energy return on the energy invested in producing them (a deal-breaking quality issue). Ocean thermal and wave power may serve coastal cities, but again the technology needs to be proven and scaled up. Coal with carbon capture and storage is economically uncompetitive with other sources of electricity. Solar and wind are getting cheaper, but they're intermittent and tend to undermine commercial utility companies' business models. While our list of potential energy sources is long, none of these sources is ready to be plugged quickly into our existing systems to provide energy in the quantity, and at the price, that the economy needs in order to continue growing.

This means that humanity's near future will almost certainly be energy-constrained. And that, in turn, will ensure that—rather than engineering nature on an ever-greater scale—we will still be depending on ecosystems that are largely beyond our control.

As a species, we've gained an impressive degree of influence over our environment by deliberately simplifying ecosystems so they will support more humans, but fewer other species. Our principal strategy in this project has been agriculture—primarily, a form of agriculture that focuses on a few annual grain crops. We've commandeered up to 50 percent of the primary biological productivity of our planet, mostly through farming and forestry.[17] Doing this has had overwhelmingly negative impacts on nondomesticated plants and animals. The subsequent loss of biodiversity is increasingly compromising humanity's prospects, because we depend upon countless ecosystem services (such as pollination and oxygen regeneration) that we do not organize or control, and for which we do not pay.

The essence of our problem is this: the side effects of our growth binge are compounding rapidly and threaten a crisis in which the artificial support systems we've built over past decades (food, transport, and financial systems, among others)—as well as nature's wild systems, on which we still also depend—could all crash more or less simultaneously.

If we've reached a point of diminishing returns and potential crisis with regard to our current strategy of constant population/consumption growth and ecosystem takeover, then it would seem that a change of direction is both necessary and inevitable. If we were smart, rather than attempting to dream up ways of further re-engineering natural systems in untested (and probably unaffordable) ways, we would be limiting and ameliorating the environmental impacts of our global industrial system while reducing our population and overall consumption levels.

If we *don't* proactively limit population and consumption, nature will eventually do it for us, and likely by very unpleasant means (famine, plague, and perhaps war). Similarly, we can rein in consumption simply by continuing to deplete resources until they become unaffordable.

Governments are probably incapable of leading a strategic retreat in our war on nature, as they are systemically hooked on economic growth.[18] But there may be another path forward. Perhaps citizens and communities can initiate a change of direction. Back in the 1970s, as the first energy shocks hit home and the environmental movement flourished, ecological thinkers began tackling the question: *What are the most biologically regenerative, least harmful ways of meeting basic human needs?* Two of these thinkers, Australians David Holmgren and Bill Mollison, came up with a system they called *permaculture*. According to Mollison, "Permaculture is a philosophy of working with, rather than against nature; of protracted and thoughtful observation rather than protracted and thoughtless labor; and of looking at plants and animals in all their functions, rather than treating any area as a single-product system."[19] Today there are thousands of permaculture practitioners throughout the world, and permaculture design courses are frequently on offer in almost every country.[20]

Other ecologists didn't aim to create an overarching system, but merely engaged in piecemeal research on practices that might lead to a more sustainable mode of food production—practices that include intercropping, mulching, and composting. One ambitious agricultural scientist, Wes Jackson of the Land Institute in Salina, Kansas, has spent the past four decades breeding perennial grain crops (he points out that our current annual grains are responsible for the vast bulk of soil erosion, to the tune of 25 billion tons per year).[21]

Meanwhile, community resilience efforts have sprung up in thousands of towns and cities around the world—including the Transition Initiatives, which are propelled by a compelling, flexible, grassroots organizing model and a vision of a future in which life is better without fossil fuels.[22]

Population Media Center is working to ensure we don't get to ten billion humans by enlisting creative artists in countries with high population growth rates (which are usually also among the world's poorest nations) to produce radio and television soap operas featuring strong female characters who successfully confront issues related to family planning. This strategy has been shown to be the most cost-effective and humane means of reducing high birth rates in these nations.[23]

What else can be done? Substitute labor for fuel. Localize food systems. Capture atmospheric carbon in soil and biomass. Replant forests and restore ecosystems. Recycle and reuse. Manufacture more durable goods. Rethink economics to deliver human satisfaction without endless growth. There are organizations throughout the world working to further each of these goals, usually with little or no government support. Taken together, they could lead us to an entirely different Anthropocene.

Call it the *Lean-Green Anthropocene*.

The Techno-Anthropocene has an Achilles heel: energy (more specifically, the failings of nuclear power). The Lean-Green Anthropocene has one as well: human nature.

It's hard to convince people to voluntarily reduce consumption and curb reproduction. That's not because humans are unusually pushy, greedy creatures; all living organisms tend to maximize their population size and rate of collective energy use. Inject a colony of bacteria into a suitable growth medium in a petri dish and watch what happens. Hummingbirds, mice, leopards, oarfish, redwood trees, or giraffes: in each instance the principle remains inviolate—every species maximizes population and energy consumption within nature's limits. Systems ecologist Howard T. Odum called this rule the Maximum Power Principle: throughout nature, "system designs develop and prevail that maximize power intake, energy transformation, and those uses that reinforce production and efficiency."[24]

In addition to our innate propensity to maximize population and consumption, we humans also have difficulty making sacrifices in the present in order to reduce future costs. We're genetically hardwired to respond to immediate threats with fight-or-flight responses, while distant hazards matter much less to us. It's not that we don't think about the future at all; rather, we unconsciously apply a discount rate based on the amount of time likely to elapse before a menace has to be faced.[25]

True, there is some variation in future-anticipating behavior among individual humans. A small percentage of the population may change behavior now to reduce risks to forthcoming generations, but the great majority is less likely to do so.[26] If that small percentage could oversee our collective future planning, we might have much less to worry about. But that's tough to arrange in democracies, where people, politicians, corporations, and even nonprofit organizations get ahead by promising immediate rewards, usually in the form of more economic growth. If none of these can organize a proactive response to long-range threats like climate change, the actions of a few individuals and communities may not be so effective at mitigating the hazard.

This pessimistic expectation is borne out by experience. The general outlines of the 21st-century ecological crisis have been apparent since the 1970s. Yet not much has actually been accomplished through efforts to avert that crisis. It is possible to point to hundreds, thousands, perhaps even millions of imaginative, courageous programs to reduce, recycle, and reuse—yet the overall trajectory of industrial civilization remains relatively unchanged.

Human nature may not permit the Lean-Greens' message to altogether avert ecological crisis, but that doesn't mean the message is pointless. To understand how it could have longer-term usefulness despite our tendency toward short-term thinking, it's helpful to step back and look at how societies' relationship with the environment tends to evolve.

The emblematic ecological crises of the Anthropocene (runaway climate change and ocean acidification, among others) are recent, but humans have been altering our environment one way or another for a long time. Indeed, there is controversy among geologists over when the Anthropocene began: some say it started with the Industrial Revolution, others tag it at the beginning of agriculture some ten thousand years ago, while still others tie it to the emergence of modern humans thousands of years earlier.

Humans have become world-changers as a result of two primary advantages: we have dexterous hands that enable us to make and use tools and we have language, which helps us coordinate our actions over time and space. As soon as both were in place, we started using them to take over ecosystems. Paleoanthropologists can date the arrival of humans to Europe, Asia, Australia, the Pacific Islands, and the Americas by noting the timing of extinctions of large prey species. The list of animals probably eradicated by early humans is long, and includes (in Europe) several species of elephants and rhinos; (in Australia) giant wombats, kangaroos, and lizards; and (in the Americas) horses, mammoths, and giant deer.[27]

People have also been deliberately re-engineering ecosystems for tens of thousands of years, principally by using fire to alter landscapes so they will produce more food for humans.[28] Agriculture was a huge boost to our ability to produce more food on less land, and therefore to grow our population. Farming yielded storable food surpluses, which led to cities—the basis of civilization. It was in these urban social cauldrons that writing, money, and mathematics emerged.

If agriculture nudged the human project forward, fossil-fueled industrialism turbocharged it. In just the past two centuries, population and energy consumption have increased by more than 800 percent. Our impact on the biosphere has more than kept pace.

The industrialization of agriculture reduced the need for farm labor. This enabled—or forced—billions to move to cities. As more people came to live in urban centers, they found themselves increasingly cut off from wild nature and ever more completely engaged with words, images, symbols, and tools.

There's a term for the human tendency to look at the biosphere, maybe even the universe, as though it's all about us: *anthropocentrism*. Up to a point, this is an understandable and even inevitable propensity. Every person, after all, is the center of her own universe, the star of his own movie; why should our species as a whole be less egocentric? Other animals are similarly obsessed with their own kind: regardless of who furnishes the kibbles, dogs are obsessively interested in other dogs. But there are healthy and unhealthy degrees of individual and species self-centeredness. When individual human self-absorption becomes blatantly destructive we call it *narcissism*. Can a whole species be overly self-absorbed? Hunter-gatherers were certainly interested in their own survival, but many indigenous forager peoples thought of themselves as part of a larger community of life, with a responsibility to maintain the web of existence.[29] Today we think more "pragmatically" (as an economist might put it) as we bulldoze, deforest, overfish, and deplete our way to world domination.

However, history is not a steady ramp-up of human hubris and alienation from nature. Periodically humans were slapped down. Famine, resource conflicts, and disease decimated populations that were previously growing. Civilizations rose, then fell. Financial manias led to crashes. Boomtowns became ghost towns.

Ecological slap-downs probably occurred relatively frequently in preagricultural times, when humans depended more directly on nature's variable productivity of wild foods. The Aboriginals of Australia and the Native Americans—who are often regarded as exemplar intuitive ecologists due to their traditions and rituals restraining population growth, protecting prey species, and affirming humanity's place within the larger ecosystem—were probably just applying lessons from bitter experience. It's only when we humans get slapped down hard a few times that we start to appreciate other species' importance,

restrain our greed, and learn to live in relative harmony with our sur-
roundings.

Which prompts the question: Are the Lean-Green Anthropocene
prophets our species' early warning system whose function is to avert
catastrophe—or are they merely ahead of their time, preadapting to
an ecological slap-down that is foreseeable but not yet fully upon us?

—— ⨳ ——

Throughout history, humans appear to have lived under two distinct regimes: boom times and dark ages. Boom times occurred in
prehistory whenever people arrived in a new habitat to discover an
abundance of large prey animals. Booms were also associated with
the exploitation of new energy resources (especially coal and oil) and
the expansions of great cities—from Uruk, Mohenjo-daro, Rome,
Chang'an, Angkor Wat, Tenochtitlan, Venice, and London, all the way
to Miami and Dubai. Boom-time behavior is risk-seeking, confident
to the point of arrogance, expansive, and experimental.

Historians use the term *dark ages* to refer to times when urban
centers lose most of their population. Think Europe in the fifth
through the fifteenth centuries, the Near East after the Bronze Age
collapse around 1200 BCE, Cambodia between 1450 and 1863 CE, or
Central America after the Mayan collapse of 900 CE. Dark-age behavior is conservative and risk-averse. It has echoes in the attitudes of
indigenous peoples who have lived in one place long enough to have
confronted environmental limits again and again. Dark-age people
haven't skirted the Maximum Power Principle; they've just learned
(from necessity) to pursue it with more modest strategies.

Needless to say, dark ages have their (ahem) dark side. In the early
phases of such periods large numbers of people typically die from
famine and war or other forms of violence. Dark ages are times of
forgetting, when technological and cultural achievements are often
lost. Writing, money, mathematics, and astronomy can all disappear.

Still, these times are not uniformly gloomy. During the European Dark Ages, slavery nearly disappeared as new farming methods

and better breeds of horses and oxen made forced human labor less economic. People who previously would have been bound in slavery became either free workers or, at worst, serfs. The latter couldn't pick up and move without their lord's permission, but generally enjoyed far more latitude than slaves. At the same time, the rise of Christianity brought new organized charitable activities and institutions, including hospices, hospitals, and shelters for the poor.[30]

Today nearly everyone in the industrialized world has adopted boom-time behavior. We are encouraged to do so by ceaseless advertising messages and by governmental cheerleaders of the growth economy. After all, we have just lived through the biggest boom in all human history—why not expect more of the same? The only significant slap-downs in recent cultural memory were the Great Depression and a couple of world wars: compared to ecological bottlenecks in ancient eras these were minor affairs; further, they were relatively brief and played out three or more generations ago. For most of us now, dark-age behavior seems quaint, pointless, and pessimistic.

It would be perverse to wish for a Great Slap-Down. Only a sociopath would welcome massive, widespread human suffering. At the same time, it is impossible to ignore these twin facts: our species' population-consumption fiesta is killing the planet, and we're not likely to end the party voluntarily.

Will we avert or face a Great Slap-Down? We're already seeing initial signs of trouble ahead in extreme weather events, high oil and food prices, and increasing geopolitical tensions. Sadly, it seems that every effort will be made to keep the party going as long as possible. Even amid unmistakable signs of economic contraction, most people will still require time to adapt behaviorally. Moreover, a slap-down likely won't be sudden and complete, but may unfold in stages. After each mini-slap we'll hear claims from boom-time diehards that techno-utopian takeoff has merely been delayed and economic expansion will soon resume, if only we follow this or that leader or political program.

But if urban centers feel the crunch and widespread techno-utopian expectations are dashed, we can expect to see evidence of profound psychological disruption. Gradually, more and more people will conclude—again, as a result of hard experience—that nature *isn't* here just for us. Whether this realization emerges from extreme weather, plagues, or resource scarcity, it will lead an ever-expanding share of the populace grudgingly to pay more attention to forces beyond human control.

Just as humans are now shaping the future of Earth, Earth will shape the future of humanity. Amid rapid environmental and social change, the message of the Lean-Greens will gain more obvious relevance. That message may not save the polar bears (though ecosystem protection programs deserve every kind of support), but it might make the inevitable transition to a new species-wide behavioral mode a lot easier. It may lead to a dark age that's less dark than it would otherwise be, one in which more of our cultural and scientific achievements are preserved. A great deal may depend on the intensity and success of the efforts of the small proportion of the population who are currently open to Lean-Green thinking—success in acquiring skills, developing institutions, and communicating a compelling vision of a desirable and sustainable post-boom society.

In the end, the deepest insight of the Anthropocene will probably be a very simple one: we live in a world of millions of interdependent species with which we have coevolved. We sunder this web of life at our peril. The Earth's story is fascinating, rich in detail, and continually self-revealing. And it's *not* all about us.

— MAY 2014

▶ CONFLICT IN THE ERA OF ECONOMIC DECLINE

MANY OF THE READERS OF MY WRITINGS, AND THOSE OF MY colleagues, have come to share a certain view of the world. It's probably fair to say that, as a group, we see resource depletion, financial chaos, and environmental disasters (principally associated with global climate change) as looming storms converging on industrial civilization. We also tend to see the unprecedented level of complexity of our society today as resulting from the historically recent energy subsidies of fossil fuels, and to a certain extent the enabling factor of debt in various forms. Thus, as the quality and quantity of our energy sources inevitably decline and financial claims melt away with the on-going burst of history's greatest credit bubble, we see a simplification and decentralization of societal systems as inevitable.

In this essay, I hope to explore some of the broader social implications of simplification and decentralization. Will wars and revolutions break out with ever-greater frequency? Will democracy thrive, or will traumatized masses find themselves at the mercy of tyrants? Will nation states survive, or will they break apart? Will regional warlords rule over impoverished and enslaved survivors? Or will local food networks and Transition groups positively transform society from the ground up?

I don't claim to have a functioning crystal ball. But tracing current trends and looking to historic analogies may help us understand our prospects better, and help us make the most of them.

The 21st Century Landscape of Conflict

Looking forward, four principal drivers of conflict are easily apparent. More may be lurking along the way.

First is the increasing prospect of *conflict between rich and poor*— i.e., between those who benefitted during history's biggest growth bash and those who provided the labor, sat on the sidelines, or were pushed aside in resource grabs.

Economic growth produces inequality as a by-product. Not only do industrialists appropriate the surplus value of the labor of their workers, as Marx pointed out, but lenders accumulate wealth from the interest paid by borrowers. We see inequality being generated by economic growth in real time in China, where roughly six hundred million people have been lifted from poverty in the last 30 years as a result of nine percent annual averaged economic growth—but where economic inequality now surpasses levels in the United States.

Just as economic growth produces winners and losers domestically, the level of wealth inequality *between* nations grows as the global economy expands. Today the disparity between average incomes in the world's richest and poorest nations is higher than ever.

The primary forces working against inequality as economies grow are government spending on social programs of all sorts, and international aid projects.

As economic growth stops, those who have benefitted the most have both the incentive to maintain their relative advantage and, in many cases, the means to do so. Which means that in a contracting economy, those who have the least tend to lose the most. There are exceptions, of course. Billionaires can in theory go broke in a matter of hours or even seconds as a result of a market crash. But in the era of "too-big-to-fail" banks and corporations, government provides a safety net for the rich more readily than for the poor.

High and increasing inequality is usually bearable during boom times, as people at the bottom of the wealth pyramid are encouraged by the prospect of its overall expansion. Once growth ceases and slips into reverse, however, inequality becomes socially unsustainable. Declining expectations lead to unrest, while absolute misery (in the sense of not having enough to eat) often results in revolution.

We've seen plenty of examples of these trends in the past few years in Greece, Ireland, Spain, the United States, and the Middle East.

In many countries, including the US, government efforts to forestall or head off uprisings appear to be taking the forms of criminalization of dissent, the militarization of police, and a massive expansion of surveillance using an array of new electronic spy technologies. At the same time, intelligence agencies are now able to employ up-to-date sociological and psychological research to infiltrate, co-opt, misdirect, and manipulate popular movements aimed at achieving economic redistribution.

However, these military, police, public relations, and intelligence efforts require massive funding as well as functioning grid, fuel, and transport infrastructures. Further, their effectiveness is limited if and when the nation's level of economic pain becomes too intense, widespread, or prolonged.

A second source of conflict consists of increasing *competition over access to depleting resources*, including oil, water, and minerals. Among the wealthiest nations, oil is likely to be the object of the most intensive struggle, since oil is essential for nearly all transport and trade. The race for oil began in the early 20th century and has shaped the politics and geopolitics of the Middle East and Central Asia; now that race is expanding to include the Arctic and deep oceans, such as the South China Sea.

Resource conflicts occur not just between nations but also within societies: witness the ongoing insurgencies in the Niger Delta, where oil revenue fuels rampant political corruption while drilling leads to environmental ravages felt primarily by the Ogoni ethnic group; see also the political infighting in fracking country here in the United

States, where ecological impacts put ever-greater strains on the social fabric. Neighbors who benefit from lease payments no longer speak to neighbors who have to put up with polluted water, a blighted landscape, and the noise of thousands of trucks carrying equipment, water, and chemicals. Eventually, however, boomtowns turn to ghost towns, and nearly everyone loses.

Thirdly, climate change and other forms of ecological degradation are likely to lead to *conflict over access to places of refuge from natural disasters*. The responsible agencies—including the United Nations University Institute for Environment and Human Security—point out that there are already 12 million environmental refugees worldwide, and that this number is destined to soar as extreme weather events increase in frequency and severity. Typically, when bad weather strikes, people leave their homes only as a last resort; in the worst instances they have no other option. As America learned during the Dust Bowl of the 1930s, when hundreds of thousands were displaced from farms in the prairies, rapid shifts in population due to forced migration can create economic and social stresses, including competition for scarce jobs, land, and resources, leading to discrimination and sometimes violence.

Where do refugees go when the world is already full? Growing economies are usually able to absorb immigrants and governments may even encourage immigration in order to keep wages down. But when economic growth ceases, immigrants are often seen as taking jobs away from native-born workers.

For this reason as well, conflict will appear both within and between countries. Low-lying island nations may disappear completely, and cross-border, weather-driven migrations will increase dramatically. Inhabitants of coastal communities will move further inland. Farmers in drought-plagued areas will pick up stakes. But can all of these people be absorbed into shantytowns in the world's sprawling megacities? Or will at least some of these cities themselves see an exodus of population due to an inability to maintain basic life-support services?

Lastly, climate change, water scarcity, high oil prices, vanishing credit, and the leveling off of per-hectare productivity and the amount of arable land are all combining to create the conditions for *a historic food crisis*, which will impact the poor first and most forcibly. High food prices breed social instability—whether in 18th-century France or 21st-century Egypt. As today's high prices rise further, social instability could spread, leading to demonstrations, riots, insurgencies, and revolutions.[1]

In summary, conflict in the decades ahead will likely center on the four factors of money, energy, land, and food. These sources of conflict will overlap in various ways. While economic inequality will not itself be *at the root of* all this conflict (one could argue that population growth is a deeper if often unacknowledged cause of strife), inequality does seem destined to *play a role* in most conflict, whether the immediate trigger is extreme weather, high food prices, or energy shortages.

This is not to say that all conflict will be over money, energy, land, or food. Undoubtedly religion will provide the ostensible banner for contention in many instances. However, as so often in history, this is likely to be a secondary rather than a primary driver of discord.

War and Peace in a Shrinking Economy

Will increasing conflict lead to expanding violence?

Not if neuropsychologist Stephen Pinker is right. In his expansive and widely praised book *The Better Angels of Our Nature: Why Violence Has Declined*, Pinker claims that, in general, violence has waned during the past few decades. He argues that this tendency has ancient roots in our shift from peripatetic hunting and gathering to settled farming; moreover, during the past couple of centuries the trend has greatly intensified. With the emergence of Enlightenment philosophy and its respect for the individual came what Pinker calls the Humanitarian Revolution. Much more recently, after World War II, violence was suppressed first by the "mutually assured destruction" policies of the two opposed nuclear-armed sides in the Cold War, and then by American global hegemony. Pinker calls this the Long Peace.

Wars have become less frequent and less violent, and most societies have seen what might be called a decline of tolerance for intolerance—whether manifested in schoolyard fights, bullying, or picking on gays and minorities.

But there is a problem with Pinker's implied conclusion that global violence will continue to decline. The Long Peace we have known since World War II may well turn out to be shorter than hoped as world economic growth stalls and American hegemony falters—in John Michael Greer's words, as "the costs of maintaining a global imperial presence soar and the profits of the imperial wealth pump slump."[2] Books and articles predicting the end of the American empire are legion; while some merely point to the rise of China as a global rival, others describe the looming failure of the essential basis of the US imperial system—the global system of oil production and trade (with its petro-dollar recycling program) centered in the Middle East. There are any number of scenarios describing how the end of empire might come, but few credible narratives explaining why it won't.

When empires crumble, as they always eventually do, the result is often a free-for-all among previous subject nations and potential rivals as they sort out power relations. The British Empire was a seeming exception to this rule: in that instance, the locus of military, political, and economic power simply migrated to an ally across the Atlantic. A similar graceful transfer seems unlikely in the case of the United States, as 21st-century economic decline will be global in scope. A better analogy to the current case might be the fall of Rome, which led to centuries of incursions by barbarians as well as uprisings in client states.

Disaster per se need not lead to violence, as Rebecca Solnit argues in her book *A Paradise Built in Hell: The Extraordinary Communities that Arise in Disaster*. She documents five disasters—the aftermath of Hurricane Katrina; earthquakes in San Francisco and Mexico City; a giant ship explosion in Halifax, Canada; and 9/11—and shows that rioting, looting, rape, and murder were not automatic results. Instead, for the most part, people pulled together, shared what resources they had, cared for the victims, and in many instances found new sources of joy in everyday life.

However, the kinds of social stresses we are discussing now may differ from the disasters Solnit surveys, in that they comprise a "long emergency," to borrow James Kunstler's durable phrase. For every heartwarming anecdote about the convergence of rescuers and caregivers on a disaster site, there is a grim historic tale of resource competition turning normal people into monsters.

In the current context, a continuing source of concern must be the large number of nuclear weapons now scattered among nine nations. While these weapons primarily exist as a deterrent to military aggression, and while the end of the Cold War has arguably reduced the likelihood of a massive release of them in an apocalyptic fury, it is still possible to imagine several scenarios in which a nuclear detonation could occur as a result of accident, aggression, preemption, or retaliation.[3]

We are in a race—but it's not just an arms race; indeed, it may end up being an arms race in reverse. In many nations around the globe the means to pay for armaments and war are starting to disappear while the incentive to engage in international conflict is increasing, as a way of rechanneling the energies of jobless young males and distracting the general populace, which might otherwise be in a revolutionary mood. We can only hope that historical momentum can maintain the Great Peace until industrial nations are sufficiently bankrupt that they cannot afford to mount foreign wars on any substantial scale.

Post-carbon Governance

Are we headed toward a more autocratic or democratic future? There's no hard and fast answer; the outcome may vary by region. However, recent history does offer some useful clues.

In his recent and important book *Carbon Democracy: Political Power in the Age of Oil*, Timothy Mitchell argues that modern democracy owes a lot to coal. Not only did coal fuel the railroads, which knitted large regions together, but striking coal miners were able to bring nations to a standstill, so their demands for unions, pensions, and better working conditions played a significant role in the creation of the modern welfare state. It was no mere whim that led Margaret Thatcher to crush the coal industry in Britain; she saw its demise as the indispensable precondition to neoliberalism's triumph.

Coal was replaced, as a primary energy source, by oil. Mitchell suggests that oil offered industrial countries a path to reducing internal political pressures. Its production relied less on working-class miners and more upon university-trained geologists and engineers. Also, oil is traded globally, so that its production is influenced more by geopolitics and less by local labor strikes. "[P]oliticians saw the control of oil overseas as a means of weakening democratic forces at home," according to Mitchell, and so it is no accident that by the late 20th century the welfare state was in retreat and oil wars in the Middle East had become almost routine. The problem of "excess democracy," which reliance upon coal inevitably brought with it, has been successfully resolved, not surprisingly by still more teams of university-trained experts—economists, public relations professionals, war planners, political consultants, marketers, and pollsters. We have organized our political life around a new organism—"the economy"—which is expected to grow in perpetuity, or, more practically, as long as the supply of oil continues to increase.

Andrew Nikiforuk also explores the suppression of democratic urges under an energy regime dominated by oil in his brilliant book *The Energy of Slaves: Oil and the New Servitude*. The energy in oil effectively replaces human labor; as a result, each North American enjoys the services of roughly 150 "energy slaves." But, according to Nikiforuk, that means that burning oil makes us slave masters—and slave masters all tend to mimic the same attitudes and behaviors, including contempt, arrogance, and impunity. As power addicts, we become both less sociable and easier to manipulate.

In the early 21st century, carbon democracy is still ebbing, but so is the global oil regime hatched in the late 20th century. Domestic US oil production based on hydraulic fracturing ("fracking") reduces the relative dominance of the Middle East petro-states, but to the advantage of Wall Street—which supplies the creative financing for speculative and marginally profitable domestic drilling. America's oil wars have largely failed to establish and maintain the kind of order in the Middle East and Central Asia that was sought. High oil prices send dollars cascading toward energy producers but starve the economy as a whole, and this eventually reduces petroleum demand. Governance systems appear to be incapable of solving or even seriously addressing looming financial, environmental, and resource issues, and "democracy" persists primarily in a highly diluted solution whose primary constituents are money, hype, and expert-driven opinion management.

In short, the 20th-century governance system is itself fracturing. So what comes next?

As the fracking boom unavoidably fails due to financial and geological constraints, a new energy regime will inevitably arise. It will almost surely be one mainly characterized by scarcity, but it will also eventually be dominated by renewable energy sources—whether solar panels or firewood. That effectively throws the door open to a range of governance possibilities. As mobility declines, smaller and more local governance systems will be more durable than empires and continent-spanning nation states. But will surviving regional and local governments end up looking like anarchist collectives or warlord compounds? Recent democratic innovations pioneered or implemented in the Arab Spring and the Occupy movement hold out more than a glimmer of hope for the former.

Anthropologist David Graeber argues that the failure of centralized governmental institutions can open the way for democratic self-organization; as evidence, he cites his own experience doing doctoral research in Madagascar villages where the state had ceased collecting taxes and providing police protection. Collecting revenues and enforcing laws are the most basic functions of government; thus these communities were effectively left to govern and provide for themselves. According to Graeber, they did surprisingly well. "[T]he people had come up with ingenious expedients of how to deal with the fact that there was still technically a government, it was just really far away. Part of the idea was never to put the authorities in a situation where they lost face, or where they had to prove that they were in charge. They were incredibly nice to [government officials] if they didn't try to exercise power, and made things as difficult as possible if they did. The course of least resistance was [for the authorities] to go along with the charade."[4]

Journalism professor Greg Downey, commenting on Graeber's ideas, notes, "I saw something very similar in camps of the Movimento Sem Terra (the MST or 'Landless Movement') in Brazil. Roadside shanty camps attracted former sharecroppers, poor farmers whose small plots were drowned out by hydroelectric projects, and other refugees from severe restructuring in agriculture toward large-scale corporate farming." These farmers were victims, but they were by no means helpless. "Activists and religious leaders were helping these communities to set up their own governments, make collective decisions, and eventually occupy sprawling ranches.... The MST leveraged the land occupations to demand that the Brazilian government adhere to the country's constitution, which called for agrarian reform, especially of large holdings that were the fruits of fraud.... [C]ommunity-based groups, even cooperatives formed by people with very little education, developed greater and greater ability to run their own lives when the state was not around. They elected their own officials, held marathon community meetings in which every member voted (even children), and, when they eventually gained land, often became thriving, tight-knit communities."[5]

A Theory of Change for a Century of Crisis

If groups seeking to make the post-carbon transition go more smoothly and equitably are to have much hope of success, they need a sound strategy grounded in a realistic theory of change. Here, briefly, is a theory that makes sense to me.

For the past four decades, since the release of *Limits to Growth*, there have been many scattered efforts to develop alternatives to our current fossil-fueled, growth-based industrial paradigm. These include renewable energy systems; local, organic, and permaculture food systems; urban design movements seeking to reduce the dominance of the automobile in our built environment; architectural programs with the goal of designing buildings that require no external energy input and that are constructed using renewable and recycled materials; alternative currencies not attached to interest-bearing debt, as well as alternative banking models; and alternative economic indicators that take account of social and environmental factors. While such efforts have achieved some small degree of implementation, varying significantly from place to place around the globe, they have generally failed to substantially reduce reliance on fossil fuels, blunt the overall momentum of society toward increased consumption, reduce financial instability, or curtail profound environmental impacts, including climate change and loss of biodiversity and topsoil.

What will it take for the conservers, localizers, and de-growthers to win? They have a lot stacked against them. The interests promoting a continuation of growth-as-usual are powerful and have spent decades honing advertising and public relations messages whose proliferation is subsidized by hundreds of billions of dollars annually. These interests have captured the allegiance of nearly every elected official in the world. Most ordinary folks are easily swept along because they want more and better jobs, cheaper gasoline, more flat-screen TVs, and all the other perks that come with fossil-fueled economic expansion.

The main downside to growth-as-usual is that it is unsustainable: it is destined to end in resource depletion, economic unraveling, and environmental catastrophe. The conservers, localizers, and de-growthers must therefore hope that if the growth-as-usual bandwagon cannot be turned back with persuasion, its inevitable crash will occur in increments, so that they can seize each step-down in industrial output as an opportunity to demonstrate and promote the need for alternatives.

Advocates of the post-carbon crisis theory of change can point to several useful historic examples. One is the transformation of Cuba's food system during that country's "Special Period" in the 1990s. The collapse of the Soviet Union and the resulting disappearance of subsidized Soviet oil shipments set the stage with a crisis. Several Cuban agronomists had previously advocated for more localized and organic agriculture, to no avail, but when the country was suddenly threatened with starvation, they were called upon to redesign the entire food system. The moral of the story: advocates of a post-carbon economy are likely to make limited headway during times of cheap energy and rapid economic growth, yet when push comes to shove obstacles may disappear. The Cuban example is encouraging, but it is often called into question on the grounds that what worked on an island with an authoritarian government might not work so well in a large, pluralistic democracy such as the United States.

Paul Gilding, in his book *The Great Disruption*, proposes World War II as an illustration of the crisis-led theory of change: "[O]n the objective facts, Hitler represented a clear and undeniable threat long before action was taken to defeat him," he writes. "Famously, Churchill and others had long warned of this threat and been largely ignored or even ridiculed. Society remained in denial, preferring not to recognize the threat. This was because denial avoided full acceptance and what that meant—war and a strong change to the status quo. Yet once… denial ended, the response was swift and dramatic. Things changed almost overnight. Without the benefit of a retrospective view, it would be much harder to predict when exactly the denial of Hitler's threat would end. So it's also hard to predict when the moment will come [when the need for action on climate change is finally recognized], even though in hindsight it will be obvious.'"

Post-Fukushima Japan offers yet another example. In the wake of catastrophic nuclear plant meltdowns, the Japanese people insisted that other reactors be idled; soon only two of the nation's atomic power plants were operating. That left Japan with substantially less electricity than normal—enough of a shortfall that economic collapse could have resulted. Instead, businesses and households slashed energy use, driven by a collective ethical imperative. Solar photovoltaic (PV) systems have appeared on rooftops across the nation.

The Kansas town of Greensburg was flattened by a tornado in May 2007, but the residents—rather than drifting away or merely trying to rebuild what they had—decided instead to use insurance and government disaster aid money to build what they are calling "America's greenest community," emphasizing energy efficiency and using 100 percent renewable energy.

Economist Milton Friedman may have laid down a manifesto for crisis-led theories of change when he wrote: "Only a crisis—actual or perceived—produces real change. When the crisis occurs, the actions that are taken depend upon the ideas that are lying around. That, I believe, is our basic function: to develop alternatives to existing policies, to keep them alive and available until the politically impossible becomes politically inevitable." In this brief passage, Friedman not only sums up the theory nicely, but also forces us to contemplate its dark side. In her 2007 book *The Shock Doctrine: The Rise of Disaster Capitalism*, Naomi Klein describes how Friedman and other neoliberal economists used crisis after crisis, beginning in the 1970s, as opportunities to undermine democracy and privatize institutions and infrastructure across the world. Somehow, citizens and communities need to be the first to seize the opportunities presented by crisis, to build local, low-carbon production and support infrastructure.

The post-carbon theory of change doesn't seek to expedite or exacerbate crisis; instead, it encourages building resilience into societal systems in order to minimize the trauma of rapid change. Resilience is often defined as "the ability to absorb shocks, reorganize, and continue functioning." Shocks are clearly on the way, so we should be doing what we can now to build local inventories and disperse the control points for critical systems. We should neither simply wait around for crisis to hit or *hope for crisis* as an opportunity to alter the status quo; rather, we should do as much as possible to conserve ecosystems and relocalize production and trade now, so as to minimize the crisis—which, after all, could potentially prove overwhelming for both humanity and nonhuman nature. If and when crisis arrives, such preparations will be crucial in guiding response efforts and providing a basis for resisting "disaster capitalism."

What's the likelihood of success? It depends partly on how we define the term in this context. Many people speak of "solving" problems like climate change, as though we could make a modest investment in new technology and then carry on living essentially as we are. Implicit in the post-carbon crisis theory of change is the understanding that the way we are living now is at the heart of our problem. Success could therefore be better defined in terms of minimizing human suffering and ecological disruption as we adapt toward a very different mode of existence characterized by greatly reduced energy and materials consumption.

Some self-proclaimed "doomers" have concluded that crisis will overwhelm society no matter what we do. Many have joined the "prepper" movement, stockpiling guns and canned goods in hopes of maintaining their own households as the rest of the world comes to resemble Cormac McCarthy's novel *The Road*. Other doomers are convinced that human extinction is inevitable and that efforts to prevent that outcome are just so much wasted motion.

I do not share either outlook. Of course there is no guarantee that crisis will open opportunities for sensible adaptation and not simply wallop us, leaving humanity and nature wounded and reeling. But for those who understand what's coming to simply give up efforts to protect nature and humanity before the going gets tough seems premature at best. There could hardly be more at stake; therefore extraordinary levels of effort and extreme persistence would appear justified if not morally mandatory. The post-carbon crisis theory of change may appear to be a strategy born of desperation. But we should hold open the possibility that it will prove surprisingly apt and effective— to the extent that we have invested our best efforts.

As we build resilience and prepare to make the most of the opportunities that come our way, it's important that we celebrate the improvements in quality of life that come with reducing our dependency on consumption, advertising, automobiles, and all the other life-smothering accoutrements of our crumbling industrial existence. Let's also celebrate our adaptability in times of crisis, and continually remind one another that small committed groups sometimes do make history—just as history makes them.

— DECEMBER 2012

▶ ALL ROADS LEAD LOCAL

CALIFORNIA IS FAMOUS FOR BEING A TRENDSETTER. BLUE jeans (San Francisco), indoor shopping malls (Los Angeles), theme parks (Anaheim), and the Internet (Silicon Valley) all got their start here.

One of the strongest current trends in Sonoma County, California, where I live, is localism. In Santa Rosa, my city, a downtown storefront is home to Share Exchange—perhaps best described as a localist mini-mall, hosting a "Made Local" marketplace, a "share space" coworking center, and a cooperative business incubator. Signs on Santa Rosa windows and lampposts advise residents to "Shop Local," "Bank Local," "Eat Local," and "Compost Local." A new county-based nonprofit power agency, Sonoma Clean Power, started up in 2014. Menus at an upscale restaurant at the center of town proclaim, "We feature organic food from local farmers." And Sonoma County is now estimated to have about 250 small commercial food producers.[1]

Of course, localism is not unique to California; it's blossoming across America, with "Go Local" programs thriving in Boston, Atlanta, Tacoma, and other cities. The US Department of Agriculture lists 8,144 farmers' markets in its National Farmers' Market Directory, up from 5,000 in 2008. Indeed, local food is one of the fastest growing segments of American agriculture, though it has yet to become as popular as blue jeans or shopping malls.

To be sure, localism has its critics, who argue that it amounts merely to a snobbish, nostalgia-driven fad; they say globalization—in effect, anti-localism—has given us economic growth and cheaper consumer goods, lifted hundreds of millions in poor countries from poverty, and contributed to cross-cultural understanding. Localism, its detractors say, rows against the tide of history.

Localism's supporters counter that globalization has spurred economic inequality and destroyed jobs. Further, localists worry that globalization is an inherently unsustainable trend that will leave households and communities high and dry when it inevitably falters. Nearly everyone agrees that global communication and cultural exchange are good things, and that complete local self-sufficiency is probably both unattainable and undesirable. Nevertheless, localists contend that, during recent decades, the economic pendulum has swung much too far toward globalism and is now poised to reverse itself, making localism the dominant trend through the remainder of this century.

Throughout this essay, as I illustrate the case for the desirability and inevitability of a return to shorter supply chains, I'll circle back to examples and evidence from my home region. Readers can readily find similar examples in their own neck of the woods. We'll also explore ways in which a localized future might challenge many of our current habits and expectations, and suggest ways enlightened policy makers could help ease the passing of globalism and the re-rooting of communities in place.

What Has Globalization Done for You Lately?

Broadly defined, globalization can be said to have a long history. The Roman Empire, the post–1492 European age of conquest, the British Empire, and the massive expansion of international trade that started in the late 20th century each brought more long-distance communication, travel, and transport of goods. All of these projects resulted in an increase of wealth for elites in urban trading centers, and mounting costs borne mostly by indigenous peoples and nonhuman species.

The last of these four great projects—for which the term *globalization* was coined—was by far the most intensive and extensive. It was driven by the convergence of key resources, developments, and inventions: cheap oil, satellite communications, container ships, computerized monitoring of inventories, the flourishing of multinational corporations, the proliferation of liberal trade treaties, and the emergence of transnational bodies such as the World Trade Organization.

For economists, globalization made perfect sense. The doctrine of comparative advantage held that if low-wage workers in Shanghai can make widgets cheaper than unionized factory employees in Camden, New Jersey, can, then widget manufacturing should move to China. And, to a large extent, it did.

Economists said everyone would eventually benefit, but casualties quickly mounted. Real wages for American workers stopped growing in the 1970s. Manufacturing towns throughout the Northeast and Midwest withered. Meanwhile, China began burning immense amounts of coal to make mountains of toys, furniture, clothing, tools, appliances, and consumer electronics, cloaking its cities in a pall of toxic fumes and driving its greenhouse gas emissions to world record-setting levels. In effect, the United States was importing cheap consumer goods while exporting jobs and pollution. In both China and the United States, levels of economic inequality soared.

These trends have direct and indirect manifestations in Sonoma County. In the first half of the 20th century my region's economy was diverse and agriculture-based. Farmers and ranchers produced a variety of foods including wheat, hops, prunes, apples, eggs, milk, and beef. Building materials were sourced from nearby forests and quarries. Today the county banks on one significant product: wine. Most of it is exported. Grapes have become an ecological blight on rural areas, where vineyards extend from horizon to horizon, crowding out ecologically diverse native oak woodlands. Wine leaves by the truckload, while everything else the people of Sonoma County need and use arrives on the backs of eighteen-wheelers—much of it from China. The vast majority of food consumed here, once locally grown, is now imported. Processed and packaged edibles available in downscale supermarkets and fast-food chain outlets in Santa Rosa are identical to what you'd find anywhere else in America these days, and contribute to rising regional rates of obesity and other food-related diseases.

California is one of the most trade-dependent states. Silicon Valley (just a couple of hours' drive south of Sonoma County) generates legendary wealth, purportedly from the groundbreaking ideas of its engineers and technicians. One of the hottest of these ideas was the smartphone, an invention that has swept the world. But the *idea* of a smartphone would amount to little without cheap labor in Asia with which to affordably manufacture hundreds of millions of these little devices, and without mines around the world churning out raw materials from which to make them.

Northern California's wealth—derived largely from globalization—draws people to live here. As a result, this area has some of the highest land prices and rents in the nation. That's not a problem if you're a high-flying tech baron or vintner; but if you work in the service industry, or are trying to make a living growing anything other than grapes, it's tough to get by.

Taking cost of living into account, California has the highest poverty rate in the country. The state is home to about 12 percent of the total US population, but a full third of US welfare recipients. Income inequality is already higher here than in almost any other state, and it's increasing fast: according to *The Economist*, in the last five years the number of Californians earning between $50,000 and $100,000 fell by almost 75,000, while income brackets above and below grew.

Project these trends a couple of decades into the future and you arrive at some version of hell—a society that is socially and ecologically ruined. A lot of Californians have already done that visualization exercise, and that's what drives them to want more local manufacturing jobs, more locally grown food, and stronger communities comprised of skilled, motivated, engaged, and decently paid people.

But the argument for localism is actually much stronger than this: even if we desperately want more cheap foreign-made goods and are happy to trade away economic equity and ecological sustainability in order to get them, globalization is a self-limiting game that has nearly run its course.

Fueling the Engine of Globalism

Without cheap transport fuel, globalization as we know it would not have been possible. True, Britain and Spain managed to build trans-oceanic empires using sails, but today's vastly larger global trade empire requires oil-fueled container ships, diesel-powered trucks and trains, and kerosene-guzzling jets and rockets (the latter to thrust communications satellites into orbit). High mobility means oil.

California is no stranger to the oil business, and the state serves as a useful case study for what's happening more broadly in the petroleum world. In the early 20th century, rows of oil derricks dotted Los Angeles, Long Beach, and Huntington Beach. Indeed, in the 1920s Standard Oil Company of California was the largest individual producer of crude oil in the United States, supplying fuel throughout the Americas.

While petroleum was California's main export throughout most of the last century, production peaked in 1985 and slowly declined. Today a pump jack still quietly sips crude behind a fence on South Mountain View Avenue in Los Angeles, while colorfully camouflaged drilling rigs bore downward on the campus of Beverly Hills High School. More drilling and production rigs are visible to drivers on Interstate 5 near Bakersfield, and on Highway 101 north of Santa Barbara. The industry still extracts half a million barrels of oil per day from beneath California's soil, but the state's current production level is less than half of what it was 30 years ago.

This is a common problem in the petroleum world: most oil-producing countries are past their prime. The ongoing depletion of giant legacy oilfields compels companies to explore in hazardous regions (such as the Arctic) or in deep water (the Gulf of Mexico), and they must rely increasingly on unconventional resources like Canada's tar sands and on technologies like hydraulic fracturing ("fracking") and horizontal drilling.

North Dakota and Texas are epicenters of the new tight oil fracking boom, but deposits amenable to fracking are present in California, too. Indeed, in 2011 the US Government's Energy Information Administration (EIA) estimated the Monterey shale formation, which underlies more than 1,700 square miles in the southern part of the state, to contain more than 15 billion barrels of "technically recoverable" oil—twice the reserves reputed for North Dakota and Texas combined.

When geoscientist David Hughes, my colleague at Post Carbon Institute, examined drilling data for California's Monterey formation in 2013, he found that initial production rates of wells are only about one-half to one-quarter those assumed by the US Government's Energy Information Administration (EIA), and total lifetime oil production per well is likely to average one-third or less of the EIA estimates. Further, the geology is far more complex and forbidding than in tight oil plays in North Dakota and Texas. The EIA's estimate of 15 billion barrels of recoverable oil in the Monterey was wildly overblown (indeed, the EIA drastically cut the Monterey forecast to six hundred million barrels in 2014).[2]

For the oil industry, big production estimates boost stock values; governments likewise thrive on economic optimism. But drill down, and the evidence suggests the current fracking boom, in California and elsewhere, is actually symptomatic of quickly diminishing returns throughout the oil sector. As such, it may be the last, brief hurrah, not just for a few overly leveraged drilling companies but for our entire petroleum-fueled, globalized way of life.

So Can We Continue Globalization Some Other Way?

We are depleting the world's naturally occurring petroleum reservoirs over a period of roughly two centuries—an eye blink in human history, but a relatively long interval in terms of most people's subjective sense of time. There is still a lot of oil left to extract and in all likelihood the world supply of transport fuel faces not a sudden shutoff but a decades-long tapering (though with ever-rising costs). Most people assume we'll just gradually shift to different sources of energy to power transport. But what's there to shift *to* that will give us the same level of mobility?

The petroleum industry proposes using natural gas more widely as a transport fuel, since shale gas (produced, like tight oil, via fracking) is currently plentiful and cheap. However, shale gas resources suffer from the same problems as tight oil—rapid per-well decline rates and limited numbers of profitable drilling sites. Touted as a bridge fuel, natural gas may in reality be a bridge to nowhere.

Electricity can power some transport, and there are more electric cars on the road today than ever before. But where will added electricity come from to keep electrified transport growing through midcentury?

The global nuclear industry is moribund. High investment costs and revised post-Fukushima risk assessments have led some nations to abandon nuclear altogether; others have scaled back plans for expansion.

Some energy analysts favor the increased use of coal, using carbon capture and storage technology (CCS, often labeled "clean coal"). Yet everywhere it has been proposed, CCS is being rejected as too costly. Without CCS, dealing with the climate crisis will require reducing global coal consumption nearly to zero by midcentury. Even if the world refuses to take climate protection seriously, there is good evidence that economically minable world coal reserves have been substantially overestimated, so coal may not be able to keep the party going much longer anyway.

Wind and solar would help solve the climate crisis, and they're renewable (though the machines used to capture energy from wind and sunlight are made from nonrenewable materials). But solar and wind have energy characteristics different from those of fossil fuels: they are intermittent and seasonal, a problem that can be solved only with major investment in energy storage or long-distance transmission. While a few analysts claim that renewables alone can power America,[3] grid operators in Germany and Spain have reported problems integrating increasing amounts of solar and wind electricity input.[4]

Electricity is not a complete transport solution even if we have enough of it. Electric airliners would be too heavy to fly even with a 40-fold increase in battery efficiency. The US military and Virgin Airlines have experimented with sophisticated aviation biofuels, but cost projections are astronomical.

For the last couple of decades, energy futurists have touted the "hydrogen economy." Former California governor Arnold Schwarzenegger liked being photographed driving his hydrogen-powered Hummer and championed the "hydrogen highway," a chain of hydrogen-equipped filling stations to service H_2-powered cars. Toyota plans to bring out a hydrogen car next year and promises to help build support infrastructure in Los Angeles and San Francisco. Yet, as of 2014, California has only nine publicly accessible hydrogen filling stations, compared to nearly ten thousand gas and diesel stations.

My state has done more than nearly any other to develop renewable energy sources and hydrogen (which, like electricity, is not an energy source in the strict sense, but an energy carrier). But the renewable energy transition is not happening remotely fast enough even here—let alone in the nation as a whole—to significantly limit climate impacts or forestall the economic consequences of oil depletion.

If we are in peril of not having enough energy to maintain transport systems at current scale, then we should urgently shift transport modes so as to maximize per-ton, per-mile fuel efficiency. Ships are the most energy-efficient haulers, then trains; trucks are much less so, while airplanes are usually the least energy-efficient means of moving people and freight. From an energy efficiency perspective, trucking—which moves the majority of US freight from factories, shipping terminals, and warehouses to stores and homes—is the weakest link in our current transport chain. We could increase transport efficiency by replacing trucks with trains in many instances, but America's rail network is incapable of taking on significant new capacity and little is being done to expand it.

Here in Santa Rosa, a city of 170,000, train tracks run through the center of town but there has been no freight or passenger service for years. The tracks are being refurbished for a diesel-powered Sonoma-Marin Area Rail Transit (SMART) passenger train, which will whisk commuters along a 70-mile corridor from Cloverdale in the north to Larkspur in the south. Limited freight service is also envisioned, using the same tracks, and there is hope for the eventual electrification of SMART, which begins service in 2016.

Meanwhile the county, with a couple of billion dollars in state and federal funding, has spent the past three years widening US Highway 101 (which bisects Santa Rosa) to six lanes, and enlarging Sonoma County Airport. In all, it is impossible to escape the conclusion that my city, county, state, and nation have bet their futures mostly on cars, trucks, airplanes, highways, and runways—and therefore, in effect, on oil. It appears to be a losing bet.

Local Dystopia, Local Utopia

The worst-case scenario for our energy and transport future is gloomy indeed: broken supply chains and a failing economy. Yet since shipping is our most fuel-efficient transport mode, globalization won't go away anytime soon just because moving product-filled containers from Guangzhou to Oakland by slow boat has gotten more expensive. High fuel prices will first impact aspects of the economy more directly dependent on cars, trucks, and airplanes. Companies will likely try to offset rising oil costs by cutting other expenses—reducing salaries and laying off workers. Economists will observe that demand for products of all kinds is falling and blame the resulting economic contraction on demographic trends, financial bubbles, deregulation, or too much regulation—anything but unaffordable oil.

We got a taste of exactly that scenario in 2008. As oil prices soared, the global financial system crumbled for apparently unrelated reasons. Trade levels plunged. Governments and central banks leapt to the rescue, boosting overall demand with deficit spending while keeping interest rates low via quantitative easing. Economic inequality increased alarmingly, but crisis was kept at bay. It's not clear how long these strategies will maintain a semblance of normalcy, as oil depletion continues inexorably to undermine the energetic basis of our global economy.

Meanwhile, climate change could nudge localization into overdrive. Imagine the following sequence of events in a not-too-distant year: During summer, severe drought hammers the Midwest; then, in early autumn, a massive hurricane devastates areas of the Gulf coast. As winter descends, epic rains flood California's Central Valley and coastal cities, rendering a million people stranded and homeless. A Republican-dominated Congress, suffering from disaster fatigue and reluctant to run up the Federal deficit, refuses to approve relief money for California. The takeaway message: continent-spanning supply chains are a terrific investment during boom years, but if and when maintenance costs mount…you're on your own.

For "doomers" and "preppers" who lie awake at night worrying about climate change and resource depletion, the failure of complex national and global provisioning systems amounts to nothing but collapse and calamity. But other futurists tell a happier predictive story about localization, and it begins with renewable energy.

Solar and wind may not be able to replicate all the payoffs of fossil fuels—which are concentrated, available on demand, and ideal for fueling centralized grid systems and vehicles of all kinds. But what if society were to play to the strengths of these new energy sources rather than trying to force-fit them into systems designed for oil, coal, and gas? The result would likely be an energy economy that is distributed, decentralized, and under local control.

The trend may already be quietly beginning: because conventional utilities have a hard time accommodating high levels of intermittent input, some are starting to penalize grid-tied rooftop solar homes. For solar homeowners, a way to avoid these financial disincentives is to go off-grid. While the required initial investment is high, renewable generating systems are cheap to run because there is no fuel cost. If off-gridding were to become widespread, the ultimate outcome would be much lower overall energy consumption levels within a national energy system that is highly diverse, localized, and even anarchic by present standards, with electricity use primarily occurring when intermittent energy is available.

Another technological development possibly leading to a happy local future is 3-D printing. Jet printers that spray particles of metal or plastic resin instead of ink, piling up layers to produce a useful object, are still relatively uncommon. But printers are evolving quickly and their price is plummeting. As applications of the technology expand, more products will be manufactured at their point of purchase or use. While per-unit production costs may be higher, reduced shipping and inventory expenditures will more than compensate. Supply chains of raw materials—from mines to printers—would be needed, and some environmentalists have legitimate concerns about the waste and toxics produced by these machines; still, studies suggest that overall materials and energy consumption would be less than is the case with our current centralized, globalized systems of production and distribution.

A complementary bit of hopeful news from the technology world comes from farmer-physicist Marcin Jacubowski and colleagues, who have spent the past few years inventing the Global Village Construction Set—open-source blueprints that enable fabrication (from locally available recycled materials) of 50 key industrial machines, including tractors, wind turbines, bioplastic extruders, and 3-D printers. Jacubowski's goal is to provide every community with access to the basic technology needed to maintain a comfortable, sustainable, locally self-sufficient existence. So far, only a few of the modular machines have been fully designed and prototyped, but Jacubowski's project has attracted both investors and eager interns.

For solution-oriented localists, these hopeful developments coalesce into a vision of a nation of small producers living in thriving cities, towns, and villages, with chickens in every backyard, solar panels on every roof, a 3-D printer on every desktop, and an open-sourced set of productive machinery in every neighborhood. In such a future, globalized communication (and hence cultural exchange) might persist, but without job losses and export of pollution.

Which will it be—local dystopia or utopia? In all likelihood, our real future will hold a bit of both. The relative mixture of the two probably depends on what we do now.

All Politics Is Local…Is Global…Is Local

Among environmentalists, the most common critique of localism is that climate change—an existential planetary threat—requires a global response. It is useless for individuals or communities to reduce CO_2 output if overall emissions from power plants and cars continue growing. If we can't achieve an international agreement to cut carbon, we're all toast—even if we're proud to be locally made, whole-grain toast.

Though I haven't conducted a proper survey, it's my impression that most localists strongly support a global climate treaty. But 20 years of efforts to hammer out a meaningful global emissions-reduction regime have so far failed. The reason is plain: slowing climate change means pouring sand in the gears of the fossil-fueled economic growth machine. Yes, coffee tables of environmental nonprofits groan under the weight of well-meaning books and reports striving to show how carbon offsets, carbon trading, and green technology could keep economies growing even as greenhouse gas emissions wane. But most such rhetoric is, in the end, politically motivated and unintentionally misleading. Climate scientist Kevin Anderson of the UK-based Tyndall Centre displays refreshing honesty in his call for planned economic recession. Anderson figures that industrial nations need to cut carbon emissions by ten percent per year to avert catastrophe, and it's pretty obvious that such rapid reduction would be, in his words, "incompatible with economic growth."[5] Ergo, let's engineer a depression.

Meanwhile, back in Washington, Beijing, and London, virtually all policy makers cling to the belief that growth is the only thing that matters. President Obama explained his priorities plainly in a news conference in November 2012: "If the message is somehow we're going to ignore jobs and growth simply to address climate change, I don't think anybody's going to go for that. I won't go for that."[6]

In effect, we environmentalists are stuck with two strategies, neither of which is working very well: the first is to double down on grand energy transition plans that promise more jobs and growth (while ignoring real economic costs); the second is to call for national policies to shrink economic throughput, knowing that no high-level policy maker is likely to sign on.

Localism offers a third approach that does not directly conflict with either of these. Simply: Let's do what we can locally to reduce consumption, thereby lessening the global carbon burden while building personal and community resilience so we can better respond to the now-unavoidable climatic and economic impacts. Typically, it's easier to change personal behavior or local ordinances than to enact national or international policies—so why not start small?

Most of the good news with regard to climate mitigation efforts is coming from small countries, states, counties, and towns anyway. Here in Sonoma County, a nonprofit called the Climate Protection Campaign has signed regional cities onto the most ambitious carbon reduction goals in the nation. Transition Network, which promotes "small-scale local responses to the global challenges of climate change, economic hardship, and shrinking supplies of cheap energy," boasts thousands of projects in 44 countries—including five in Sonoma County.[7] Many more examples could be cited.

Since localization efforts often target reducing consumption as one of their subsidiary goals, policy makers actually have a disincentive to support such efforts. After all, if everyone were to reduce spending the economy would contract and tax revenues would shrink.

Just as some policy makers have better climate scorecards than others, we can expect that some will be more (or less) supportive of localization. State, county, and city officials need to be reminded that money spent in local businesses tends to stay in local communities and gets recycled three times more than money spent at chain stores.[8]

The path to a more localized future holds both promise and peril. There are lots of clues and opportunities we can grasp now to help us realize promise and minimize peril later on. We're more likely to recognize those clues and opportunities as we begin to pay better attention to our neighbors, our regional history, and our local ecology. Our sustenance and survival will increasingly depend on relationships with the people and natural systems around us; as we nourish and protect them, they will have greater capacity to do the same for us.

— IN PRESS

▶ OUR EVANESCENT CULTURE

– AND THE AWESOME DUTY OF LIBRARIANS

How secure is our civilization's accumulated knowledge? It is a question that, in a fundamental sense, transcends many of the life-and-death concerns (threats of sickness, natural disaster, or military invasion) that prompt us to spend fortunes on insurance, health care, and weaponry. We know that we each individually will die, though we are willing to go to great lengths to delay the event as long as possible. But we have an overarching shared interest in making sure that the world of ideas will go on without us: that our descendants will continue to compose music, invent tools, refine scientific knowledge, and write histories, extending into the indefinite future the cumulative, constantly evolving universe of signs, symbols, and skills that have enriched our lives. Cultural death—the passing of the wisdom, artistic creations, and practical knowledge of an entire people, painstakingly built up over many generations—is a loss almost too wrenching to contemplate.

Yet cultures do die. The examples from history are legion. Anthropologists and archaeologists have identified more than ten thousand distinct human cultures, most of which have perished, many by absorption into one multiethnic civilization or another. Linguists have catalogued more than six thousand human languages; again, most are extinct or endangered, often for a similar reason—absorption of indigenous populations into multiethnic urban civilizations. But civilizations are also mortal: about 24 are known to have existed over the past few thousand years, and again, most are now dust.

Here is perhaps the most salient fact: when past civilizations were in the process of decline and collapse, they seem to have given insufficient thought to preserving the best of their achievements. Indeed, the reverse often happened—libraries were burned, statues defaced, tombs looted. Archaeologists make heroic efforts to piece together the histories of these vanished empires, but they face enormous hurdles. Even the monumental and long-lasting civilization of ancient Egypt left behind more questions about itself than answers: we're not even sure how much arithmetic and geography the average educated Egyptian knew.

It might seem that our own civilization's achievements are less vulnerable. After all, the sheer weight, volume, and variety of contemporary cultural materials is unprecedented, including hundreds of millions of books and more hundreds of millions of newspapers, magazines, paintings, sculptures, photographs, motion picture films, phonograph records, CDs, DVDs, websites, and on and on.

But all this volume and diversity may be deceptive. In some respects our culture is arguably more ephemeral than most others, and a surprisingly large proportion of our cultural materials is in danger of being swept away with astonishing speed, leaving virtually no trace—like a candle flame vanishing in a puff of wind. The Egyptians carved their thoughts in enduring stone; we post ours on websites that change with lightning speed and sometimes vanish altogether.

If we want future generations to have the benefit of our achievements, we should start thinking more seriously about what to preserve, and how to preserve it.

The Ascendancy of Electronic Media

The survival struggle of America's remaining newspapers is symptomatic of a trend that began in the 1970s, when computers started finding their way into businesses, schools, and homes. Today most of us already get our news from the screen, not the local print daily—and the trend is growing. Just about every newspaper now has a website to accompany its print edition—and many industry forecasters say the print editions may not survive much longer. Even before the beginning of the Great Recession, newspaper advertising revenues were declining steeply, and in 2009 alone daily average circulation for 395 newspapers fell 7.1 percent to 34.4 million (from 37.1 million in 2008).[1] In recent years the *Rocky Mountain News* and the *Seattle Post-Intelligencer* have ceased print news operations, and both the *Chicago Sun-Times* and the *Chicago Tribune* have filed for bankruptcy. Others—like the New Orleans *Times-Picayune*, the *Detroit Free Press*, and *Detroit News*—have cut back their publishing schedule to only a few days per week or reduced the number of pages in the average edition.[2]

The magazine and book trades are likewise evolving quickly under pressure from the Internet. More than three hundred thousand new book titles still appear in the United States each year, and the book industry's sales revenue continues to grow;[3] however, many insiders think advances in digital publishing will force an unprecedented transformation of the industry, as ever fewer books are released in print versions and more in online or ebook formats—a trend already sweeping the academic textbook market.

As with newspapers, most magazines now publish their content online, and some (like *The Ecologist*) have already gone all-electronic, jettisoning their print versions. Perhaps the most economically secure of print publications are also the most ephemeral in their content—*People* magazine and other fixtures of the supermarket checkout line. And the production processes for books, magazines, and newspapers—from writing to typesetting, printing, and distribution—are already thoroughly computerized.

Digitization has nearly completed its takeover of the motion picture, photography, and music industries. Just try to buy a package of Kodachrome film for your 35-millimeter camera, or an analog recording of your favorite band's latest songs.[4] And with the explosive growth of online streaming and downloading services for music, movies, and television programming, the Internet is gradually becoming the primary delivery medium for visual and audio media.

Libraries are being forced to adapt, as they face enormous pressure to expand digital media at the expense of traditional media. For archivists, the emerging trend can be summarized in one word: *digitization.* Whether the original exists on paper, vinyl, or celluloid, its future lies in endless strings of ones and zeroes encoded on magnetic or laser-etched media, which will presumably preserve the original content while making it accessible to millions or billions of people today and in future generations.

At the same time, the very function of libraries is up for grabs: a presentation at the 2008 American Library Association conference reported in *Library Journal* suggested that libraries should be "more and more a place to do stuff, not just to find stuff. We need to stop being a grocery store and start being a kitchen."[5] As libraries become multipurpose cultural centers (in many occasions serving as informal daytime homeless shelters), one of their primary practical functions is the provision of free public Internet access, with computer included. Yet these new demands and functions arrive at a time when funding for libraries is shrinking, as city and state budgets are downsized to fit evaporating tax revenues.

Preservation of digitized knowledge can become a problem simply because of obsolescence. Think of the billions of floppy disks manufactured and encoded during the years between 1980 and 2000: few of us still have working computers capable of retrieving the data on those disks. Physical degradation is a threat as well, for both magnetic and laser-etched media.[6] But these are hardly the worldwide information system's point of greatest vulnerability.

Ultimately the entire project of digitized cultural preservation depends on one thing: electricity. As soon as the power goes off, access to the Internet goes down. CDs and DVDs become meaningless plastic disks; ebooks become inscrutable and useless; digital archives become as illegible as cuneiform tablets—in fact, more so. Digitization represents a huge bet on society's ability to keep the lights on forever.

Without precious kilowatts, what would survive? Sculpture and architecture would persist. Previous generations of sound and visual media might be decipherable: old phonograph records could still be made to emit music, given a hand crank, needle, and megaphone, and silent films would be relatively easy to show. Books and collections of physical newspapers and magazines would fare reasonably well for a few decades, but deteriorating acid-laden paper threatens the survival of about 85 percent of books and nearly 100 percent of newspapers and magazines (ancient books written on parchment and acid-free paper could last many more centuries).

It's ironic to think that the cave paintings of Lascaux may be far more durable than photos from the Hubble space telescope.

If the lights were to go out now, in just a century or two the vast majority of our recently recorded knowledge would be gone or inaccessible.

How Likely Is Blackout?

If we could be fully confident that a more-or-less permanent blackout is unthinkable, then this discussion would be a purely academic exercise. Where might such confidence come from?

Two questions could help us assess the magnitude of risk: *What has to go wrong for the lights to go out?*, and, *What has to go right for them to stay on?*

Here's a short list of what would have to go wrong:

+ Failure to replace aging infrastructure. All knowledgeable observers agree that North America's electricity grid system is overdue for a massive upgrade. According to electrical industry consultant Jason Makansi in his 2007 book *Lights Out: The Electricity Crisis, the Global Economy, What It Means to You,* "You almost can't read a report on the US electricity industry that doesn't decry the state of the nation's transmission grid." The consequences of failure to invest tens of billions in new infrastructure will be more frequent and ever-longer blackouts and brownouts, leading perhaps to electricity rationing and a host of fairly dire economic impacts.

+ Unavailability of sufficient investment capital. Replacing infrastructure will require capital and political will. The current grid was built when energy was cheap, demand for electricity was lower, and the economy was growing at a rapid pace. Today investment capital is scarce, so the federal government will have to pay for most of the grid upgrade. But the US budget is already overextended in paying for bailout and stimulus packages, not to mention a globe-spanning military presence. Until an unavoidable crisis arises, grid investment is likely to continue being moved back in the line of projects needing money.

+ Inability of the industry to maintain sufficient supplies of fossil fuels for electricity generation. In my 2009 book *Blackout*, I discussed credible reports suggesting that US coal production could peak in the years between 2020 and 2030 and decline afterward, with prices for the resource inevitably escalating. Natural gas seems plentiful for the time being, but continued exploration and production from new shale gas plays require high gas prices; further, problems with well productivity, limits to potential drilling locations, and low energy return on energy invested may render the new shale gas plays a mere flash in the pan, as I argued in my 2013 book *Snake Oil: How Fracking's False Promise of Plenty Imperils Our Future.*

+ Inability of alternatives to make up for fossil fuels. If higher-priced and soon-to-be scarce coal and gas could be easily, quickly, and cheaply replaced with other energy sources, fossil fuel supply limits would pose no great difficulty. However, all of the available alternatives are inadequate in one way or another. Yes, we could have more wind, solar, geothermal, and tidal power—but it will take time and enormous amounts of investment capital (see above), and most of these alternatives are intermittent energy sources. And with transport of workers, fuel, and waste compromised by oil depletion, and availability of cooling water rendered unpredictable by droughts and floods associated with climate change, nuclear power will become more of a problem than a solution.[7]

+ Nuclear war. The electromagnetic pulse generated by the explosion of hydrogen bombs has the capacity to fry the grid, and the hundreds of millions of electrical devices plugged into it, nearly instantaneously. For war planners, this possibility is not only real and credible, it is one of the greatest causes of worry with regard to national survival following any nuclear exchange.

+ Solar pulse, geomagnetic storm. Under rare circumstances, an extremely intense solar flare has the capability of wiping out electricity grids across entire continents. In 1989, one such storm caused a blackout across Quebec. The largest recorded geomagnetic storm, often referred to as the Carrington Event, occurred on September 1–2, 1859. Telegraph wires in both the United States and Europe lit up, in some cases shocking telegraph operators and causing fires. If an event of similar magnitude were to occur today, millions of electronic devices would be permanently damaged, along with crucial high-voltage transformers that maintain electricity grids. A similar-intensity solar eruption aimed at our planet will inevitably occur at some point.[8]

+ Systemic vulnerabilities. We live in a world that is increasingly interconnected, and in which the pursuit of economic efficiency has reduced overall resilience. In such a system, problems in one area have a way of spilling over to create more problems elsewhere. For example, difficulties with oil supply will also eventually impact the electricity system, since spare parts and fuel (especially coal) for that system are made and/or transported with oil; similarly, problems with the electric grid will impact oil supply, since pumps and refineries require alternating current. Natural disasters, sabotage, social breakdown, and economic collapse could have knock-on effects (some too circuitous to predict) that would imperil continued, reliable delivery of electrical power.

What has to go *right* in order to avert grid breakdown? In many respects, this list is a mirror image of the previous one:

+ Successful massive investments in grid upgrades. As discussed above, these are far from being assured.
+ A rapid, successful conversion to alternative energy sources. Again, as mentioned above, this is a long shot at best.
+ Averting of international conflicts that might go nuclear. So far, so good....
+ Averting of grid breakdowns due to natural disasters, etc., or rapid recovery from such problems. Society has been able to do this for decades: even in the cases of hurricanes, earthquakes, and wars, recovery was usually rapid. But increasingly crises are becoming synergetic.

The breakdown of electricity supply systems is not just a matter of theory. In about a hundred nations around the globe, supplies of power are already problematic. Consider just one example: the nuclear-armed nation of Pakistan. Here is a quote from an article posted a few years ago on the website *All Things Pakistan*:

> While rolling blackouts or load shedding as it's locally known has always been a staple of daily life in Pakistan, the problem has become acute in the last couple of years. In the second half of December, the situation got so bad that WAPDA & KESC [power generation entities in Pakistan] resorted to draconian levels of load shedding. The power cuts during this time amounted to 20–22 hours a day in most small cities and even cities like Karachi were seeing 18+ hours of load shedding.[9]

Pakistan is a poor, politically unstable country; surely nothing like this could ever happen in a wealthy industrial nation! Yet consider the situation in Britain: a 2009 article in the *Telegraph* was headlined, "Britain Heading Back to the Dark Ages: The UK is facing a tipping point over the next few years in its ability to generate enough power to satisfy an ever-increasing demand."[10] The article notes: "Over the next 10 years, one third of Britain's power-generating capacity needs to be replaced with cleaner fuels, as a result of European laws on pollution. By 2025 the situation is expected to worsen…." Another article, this one from the BBC, is titled, "Britain Could Face Blackouts by 2016";[11] it quotes David MacKay, a researcher at Cambridge University and soon-to-be government energy advisor, as saying, "The scale of building required [to avert blackouts] is absolutely enormous."

Generating electricity is not all that difficult in principle; people have been doing it since the 19th century. But generating it in large amounts, reliably, without both cheap energy inputs and secure availability of spare parts and investment capital for maintenance, poses an increasing challenge.

To be sure, here in the United States the lights are unlikely to go out all at once, and permanently, any time soon. The most likely scenario would see a gradual increase in rolling blackouts and other forms of power rationing, beginning a decade or two from now, with some regions better off than others. After another few years, unless governments and utilities could muster the needed effort, electricity might increasingly be seen as a luxury. Reliable, ubiquitous, 24/7 power could become just a dim memory. If the challenges noted above are not addressed, many nations, including the United States, could be in such straits by the third decade of the century.

In the best instance, nations would transition as much as possible to renewable power, maintaining a functioning national grid or network of local distribution systems but supplying rationed power in smaller amounts than is the currently the case. Digitized data would still be retrievable part of the time, by some people. Yet even distributed renewable energy systems and commercial-scale fuel cells (already being used as backups for major buildings) would be vulnerable to lack of spare parts and thus might leave communities without power for extended periods. While the Internet is designed to survive if sections of the network are destroyed, the server farms that are its backbone require enormous amounts of electricity, as do the countless servers hosting private websites. Thus even if your own forward-thinking neighborhood manages to stay powered 24/7 with solar panels and methane digesters, the servers that had once stored years of your email correspondence, family photos, and financial records may be sitting dark and dead in buildings thousands of miles away.

(Indeed, if you want to know the future of the Internet, don't look to Google or Microsoft; look instead to Greece, Spain, Nigeria, or Kenya, where people with little money make the most of limited online access. Maintaining the benefits of global communications in a time of scarcity will depend, not on our willingness to constantly update hardware and software, but on our ability to maintain the functionality of an aging set of devices using as few energy, financial, and other resources—and as little bandwidth—as possible.)

In the worst instance, economic and social crises, wars, fuel shortages, and engineering problems would rebound upon one another, creating a snowballing pattern of systemic failures leading to permanent, total blackout. It may seem inconceivable that it would ever come to that. After all, electrical power means so much to us that we assume the officials in charge will do whatever is necessary to keep the electrons flowing. But, as Jared Diamond documents in his book *Collapse*, elites don't always do the sensible thing even when the alternative to rational action is universal calamity.

Altogether, the assumption that long-term loss of power is unthinkable just doesn't stand up to scrutiny. A permanent blackout scenario should exist as a contingency in our collective planning process.

Remember Websites?

Over the short term, if the power were to go out, loss of cultural knowledge would not be at the top of most people's lists of concerns. They would worry about more mundane necessities like refrigeration, light, heat, and banking. It takes only a few moments of reflection (or an experience of living through a natural disaster) to appreciate how many of life's daily necessities and niceties would be suddenly absent.

Of course, everyone did live without power until only a few generations ago, and hundreds of millions of people worldwide still manage in its absence. So it is certainly possible to carry on the essential aspects of human life *sans* functioning wall outlets. One could argue that, post-blackout, there would be a period of adaptation, during which people would reformulate society and simply get on with their business—living perhaps in a manner similar to their 19th-century ancestors or the contemporary Amish.

The problem with that reassuring picture is that we have come to rely on electrical power for so many things—and have so completely let go of the knowledge, skills, and machinery that could enable us to live without it—that the adaptive process might not go well. The survivors might not be able to attain a 19th-century way of life without spending years, decades, or perhaps even centuries reacquiring knowledge and skills and reinventing machinery.

Imagine the scene, perhaps two decades from now. After years of gradually lengthening brownouts and blackouts, your town's power has been down for days, and no one knows if or when it can be restored. No one is even sure if the blackout is statewide or nationwide, because radio broadcasts have become sporadic. The able members of your community band together to solve the mounting practical problems threatening your collective existence. You hold a meeting.

Someone brings up the problems of water delivery and wastewater treatment: the municipal facilities require power to supply these essential services. A woman in the back of the room speaks: "I once read about how you can purify water with a ceramic pot, some sand, and charcoal. It's on a website…." Her voice trails off. *There are no more websites.*

The conversation turns to food. Now that the supermarkets are closed (no functioning lights or cash registers) and emptied by looters, it's obviously a good idea to encourage backyard and community gardening. But where should townspeople get their seeds? A middle-aged gentleman pipes up: "There's this great mail-order seed company—just go online…." He suddenly looks confused and sits down.

"Online" is a world that no longer exists. Even if an order could somehow be placed, the local post office has closed its doors and its delivery trucks have run out of fuel because gas station pumps need electricity to operate.

Is There Something We Should Be Doing?

There is a message here for leaders at all levels of government and business—obviously so for emergency response organizations. But I've singled out librarians in this essay because they may bear the gravest responsibility of all in preparing for the possible end of electric civilization.

Without widely available practical information, recovery from a final blackout would be difficult in the extreme. Therefore it is important that the kinds of information people would need are identified and preserved in such a way that it will be accessible under extreme circumstances, and to folks in widely scattered places.

Of course, librarians can never bear sole responsibility for cultural preservation; *it takes a village,* as Hillary Clinton once proclaimed in another context. Books are clearly essential to cultural survival, but they are just inert objects in the absence of people who can read them; we also need skills-based education to keep alive both the practical and the performing arts. What good is a set of parts to the late Beethoven string quartets—arguably the greatest music our species has ever produced—if there's no one around who can play the violin, viola, or cello well enough to make sense of them? And what good would a written description of horse-plowing do to a post-industrial farmer without the opportunity to learn hands-on from someone with experience?

Nevertheless, for librarians the message could not be clearer: Don't let books die. It's understandable that librarians spend much effort trying to keep up with the digital revolution in information storage and retrieval: their main duty is to serve their community *as it is,* not a community that existed decades ago or one that may exist decades hence. Yet the thought that they may be making the materials they are trying to preserve ever more vulnerable to loss should be cause for pause.

There is a task that needs doing: the conservation of essential cultural knowledge in non-digital form. This task will require the sorting and evaluation of information for its usefulness to cultural survival—triage, if you will—as well as its preservation. It may be unrealistic to expect librarians to take on this responsibility, given their existing mandate and lack of resources—but who else will do it? Librarians catalog, preserve, and make available accumulated cultural materials, especially those in written form. That's their job. What profession is better suited to accept this charge?

The contemplation of electric civilization's collapse can't help but provoke philosophical musings. Perhaps cultural death is a necessary component of evolution, like the death of individual organisms. In any case, no one can prevent culture from changing, and many aspects of our present culture arguably deserve to disappear (we each probably carry our own list around in our head of what kinds of music, advertising messages, and television shows we think the world could do without). Even assuming that humans survive the current century—by no means a sure thing—another culture will arise sooner or later to replace our current electric civilization. Its cocreators will inevitably use whatever skills and notions are at hand to cobble it together (just as the inhabitants of Europe in the Middle Ages and the Renaissance drew upon cultural flotsam from the Roman Empire as well as influences from the Arab world), and it will gradually assume a life of its own. Still, we must ask: *What cultural ingredients might we want to pass along to our descendants? What cultural achievements would we want to be remembered by?*

Civilization has come at a price. Since the age of Sumer, urbanization has been terrible for the environment, leading to deforestation, loss of topsoil, and reduced biodiversity. There have been human costs as well, in the forms of economic inequality (which hardly existed in pre-state societies) and loss of personal autonomy. These costs have grown to unprecedented levels with the advent of industrialism—civilization on amphetamines—and have been borne primarily not by civilization's beneficiaries but by other species and people in poor nations and cultures. But nearly all of us who are aware of these costs like to think of this bargain-with-the-devil as having some purpose greater than a temporary increase in creature comforts, safety, and security for a minority within society. The full-time division of labor that is the hallmark of civilization has made possible science—with its enlightening revelations about everything from human origins to the composition of the cosmos. The arts and philosophy have developed to degrees of sophistication and sublimity that escape the descriptive capacity of words.

Yet so much of what we have accomplished, especially in the last few decades, currently requires for its survival the perpetuation and growth of energy production and consumption infrastructure, which exact a continued, escalating environmental and human toll. At some point, this all has to stop, or at least wind down to some more sustainable scale of pillage.

But if it does, and in the process we lose the best of what we have achieved, will it all have been for nothing?

— OCTOBER 2009

14

▶ OUR COOPERATIVE DARWINIAN MOMENT

EVOLUTION CAN BE RUTHLESS AT ELIMINATING THE UNFIT. "RED in tooth and claw," as Tennyson memorably described it, Nature routinely sacrifices billions of individual organisms and sometimes entire species in the course of its adaptive progression.

We humans have been able to blunt Nature's fangs. We take care of individuals who would not be able to survive on their own—the elderly, the sick, the wounded—and we've been doing so for a long time, perhaps tens of thousands of years.[1] In recent decades more and more of us have leapt aboard the raft of socially ensured survival—though in ways that often have little to do with compassion: today even most hale and hearty individuals would be hard pressed to stay alive for more than a few days or weeks if cut adrift from supermarkets, ATMs, and the rest of the infrastructure of modern hyper-industrialism.

This strategy of expanding our collective fitness has (at least temporarily) paid off: the consequent reduction in our death rate has resulted in a 700-percent expansion of human population in just the past two centuries and a current population growth rate of about 80 million per year (births in excess of deaths). Humans are everywhere taking carrying capacity away from most other organisms, except ones that directly serve us such as maize and cattle. We have become expert at cooperatively avoiding nature's culling, and thus at partially (and, again, temporarily) defeating natural selection—at least, in the way it applies to other species.

Some argue that "natural selection" is at work within human society whenever clever and hardworking folks get ahead while lazy dullards lag behind. The philosophy of Social Darwinism holds that this kind of competitive selection improves the species. But critics point out that individual success within society can be maladaptive for society as a whole because if wealth becomes too unequally distributed, social stability is threatened. Such concerns have led most nations to artificially limit competitive selection at the societal level: in the United States, these limits take the forms of progressive income tax, Social Security, food stamps, disability payments, Medicaid, and Aid for Dependent Children, among others. Even most self-described "conservatives" who think that government shouldn't prevent society's winners from taking all still think it's good for churches to give to the needy.

While the last few decades of rapid economic growth and material abundance—enabled by cheap fossil energy—led to a dramatic expansion of social safety nets in industrialized countries, they also featured the emergence of an ostensibly benign global imperial system led by the United States, whose fearsome military machine kept a lid on international conflict and whose universally accepted currency helped maintain relative international economic stability (in ways that served US interests, of course). Globally, deaths from war have declined, as has mortality linked to dire poverty.

So far, so good (more or less).

Unfortunately, however, many key components of our successful collective efforts to beat the Reaper are essentially unsustainable. We have reduced mortality not just with antibiotics (to which microbes eventually develop immunity) but also with an economic strategy of drawing down renewable resources at rates exceeding those of natural replenishment, and of liquidating nonrenewable resources as quickly as possible. By borrowing simultaneously from the past (when fossil fuels were formed) and the future (when our grandchildren will have to clean up our mess, pay our debt, and do without the resources we squander), we are effectively engaging in population *overshoot*.[2] Every population ecologist knows that when a species temporarily overshoots its environment's long-term carrying capacity, a die-off will follow.

And so, as the world economy stops growing and starts contracting in the coming years, the results will likely include a global increase in human mortality.[3]

Resilience theorists would say we're entering the "release" phase of the adaptive cycle that characterizes all systemic development, a phase they describe as "a rapid, chaotic period during which capitals (natural, human, social, built, and financial) tend to be lost and novelty can succeed."[4] This is a notion to which we'll return repeatedly throughout this essay, and it's a useful way of conceptualizing an experience that, for those undergoing it, will probably feel a lot less like "release" and more like "pure hell." Among the possible outcomes: Government-funded safety nets become unaffordable and are abandoned. Public infrastructure decays. Economic systems, transport systems, political systems, health care systems, and food systems become inoperable to varying degrees and in a variety of ways. Global military hegemony becomes more difficult to maintain for a range of reasons (including political dysfunction and economic decline at the imperial core, scarcity of transport fuel, and the proliferation of cheap but highly destabilizing new weapons) and international conflict becomes more likely. Any of those outcomes increases our individual vulnerability. Everyone on the raft is imperiled, especially those who are poor, old, sick, or disabled.

We could redesign our economic, political, transport, health care, and food systems to be less brittle. But suggestions along those lines have been on the table for years and have been largely rejected because they don't serve the interests of powerful groups that benefit from the status quo. Meanwhile the American populace seems incapable of raising an alarm or responding to one, consisting as it does of a large underclass that is overfed but undernourished, overentertained but misinformed, overindebted and underskilled; and a much smaller overclass that lives primarily by financial predation and is happy to tune out any evidence of the dire impacts of its activities.

A thoroughly unsentimental reader of the portents might regard an increase in the human death rate as an inevitable and potentially beneficial culling of the species. The unfit will be pruned away, the fit will survive, and humanity will be the better for it. Eventually. In theory.

Or maybe the rich and ruthless will survive and everyone else will either perish or submit to slavery.

The greatest danger is that, if social support systems utterly fail, "overshoot" could turn to "undershoot": that is, population levels could overcorrect to the point that there are fewer survivors than there *could have been* if adaptation had been undertaken proactively—perhaps far fewer than the population just prior to the Industrial Revolution. And for those who do manage to struggle on, levels of culture and technology might plummet to a depth far below what could have been preserved had action been taken.

We have a population bottleneck, as William Catton calls it, ahead of us no matter what we do at this point.[5] Even if a spectacular new energy source were to appear tomorrow, it would do little more than buy us a bit of time before we bumped up against another natural limit. However, we still get to choose *how* to pass through that bottleneck. We can exert some influence on factors that will determine how many of us get through, and in what condition.

Cooperative or Competitive Adaptation

A worst-case scenario is likely to be averted only by an effective, cooperative effort to adapt to scarcity and to recover from crises.

Fortunately there are perfectly good reasons for assuming that collaborative action along these lines will in fact emerge. We are a supremely cooperative species, and even our earliest ancestors were dedicated communitarians. Other species, though they often squabble over food and potential mates, likewise engage in sharing and cooperative behavior.[6] Members of one species sometimes even cooperate with or offer help to members of different species.[7] Indeed, as evolutionary theorist Peter Kropotkin pointed out in his landmark 1902 book *Mutual Aid*, evolution is driven by cooperation as much as by competition.[8]

More to the point, hard times can bring out the worst in people, but also the best. Rebecca Solnit argues in *A Paradise Built in Hell*[9] that people tend to cooperate, share, and help out at least as much during periods of crisis as during times of plenty. A critic might suggest that Solnit stretches this argument too far, and that collapsing societies often feature soaring rates of crime and violence (see, for example, Argentina circa 2000); nevertheless, she supports her thesis with compelling examples.

Assuming we fail to *prevent* crisis and merely *respond* to it, we might nevertheless anticipate a range of possible futures, depending on whether we set ourselves up to compete or cooperate. At one end of the competitive-cooperative scenarios spectrum, the rich few become feudal lords while everybody else languishes in direst poverty. At the other end of that spectrum, communities of free individuals cohere to produce necessities and maximize their chances for collective prosperity. Back at the "competitive" end of the scale, there is hoarding of food and widespread famine, while at the "cooperative" extreme community permaculture gardens spring up everywhere. With more competition, people perish for lack of basic survival skills; with more collaboration, people share skills and care for those with disabilities of one kind or another. Competitive efforts by investors to maintain their advantages could lead to a general collapse of trust in financial institutions, culminating in the cessation of trade at almost every level; but with enough cooperation, people could create a non-growth-based monetary system that acts as a public utility, leading to a new communitarian economics.

It's a Setup

In the real world, humans are both competitive and cooperative—always have been, always will be. But circumstances, conditioning, and brain chemistry can tend to make us more competitive or more collaborative. As we pass through the population-resource-economy bottleneck in the decades ahead, competitive and cooperative behaviors will in turn come to the fore in various times and places. My initial point in all of this is that, even in the absence of effective action to *avert* economic and environmental crises, we still have the capacity to set ourselves up to be either more competitive or more cooperative in times of scarcity and crisis. With the right social structures and the right conditioning, whole societies can become either more cutthroat or more amiable.[10] By building community organizations now, we are improving our survival prospects later.

But I'd go further. Here's a preliminary hypothesis for which I'm starting to collect both confirming and disconfirming evidence: We're likely to see the worst of ruthless competition in the early stage of the release phase, when power holders try to keep together what wants to fall apart and reorganize. The effort to hang on to what we have in the face of uncertainty and fear may bring out the competitive nature in many of us, but once we're in the midst of actual crisis we may be more likely to band together.

Among elites—who have enormous amounts of wealth, power, and privilege at stake—the former tendency has carried the day. And since elites largely shape the rules, regulations, and information flows within society, this means we're all caught up in a hyper-competitive and fearful moment as we wait for the penny to drop. Elites can deliberately nurture an "us-versus-them" mentality (via jingoistic patriotism, wedge issues, and racial resentments) to keep ordinary people from cooperating more to further their common interests.[11] Revolution, after all, is in many respects a cooperative undertaking, and in order to forestall it rulers sometimes harness the cooperative spirit of the masses in going to war against a common foreign enemy.

The over-competitiveness of this prerelease phase is playing out most prominently and fatefully in debates over "austerity," as nations bail out investment banks while leaving most citizens to languish under layoffs, pension cuts, and wage cuts. It seems that no measure aimed to prevent defaults and losses to investors is too draconian. But in many historic instances (Russia, Iceland, Argentina) it was only *after* a massive financial default—that is, once release had run its course—that nations could fundamentally revamp their monetary and banking systems, making recovery possible. That makes "release" sound a bit like a long-overdue vacation. It's important to emphasize, however, that what we face now is not just a collapse and reorganization of a national financial sector, but a crucial turning from the overall expansionary trajectory of civilization itself.

Our collective passage through and reorganization after the release phase of this pivotal adaptive cycle can be thought of as an evolutionary event. And, as noted above, evolution is driven by cooperation as much as by competition. Indeed, cooperation is the source of most of our species' extraordinary accomplishments so far. Language—which gives us the ability to coordinate our behavior across space and time—has made us by far the most successful large animal species on the planet. Our societal evolution from hunting-and-gathering bands to agrarian civilizations to industrial globalism required ever-higher levels of cooperative behavior: as one small example, think for a moment about the stunningly rich collaborative action required to build and inhabit a skyscraper. As we adapt and evolve further in the decades and centuries ahead, we will do so by finding even more effective ways to cooperate.

Ironically, however, during the past few millennia, and especially during the most recent century, social complexity has permitted greater concentrations of wealth, thus more economic inequality, and hence (at least potentially) more competition for control over heaps of agglomerated wealth. As Ivan Illich pointed out in his 1974 classic *Energy and Equity*, there has been a general correlation between the amount of energy flowing through a society and the degree of inequality within that society.[12] And so, as we have tapped fossil fuels to permit by far the highest energy flow rates ever sustained by any human civilization, a few individuals have accumulated the biggest pots of wealth the world has ever seen. Perhaps it should come as no surprise that it is precisely during this recent, aberrant, high-energy historic interval that Social Darwinism and neoliberal economics have arisen, with the latter coming to dominate economic and social policy worldwide.

The Leap

With release will come the opportunity for a collaborative evolutionary surge. Recall that in the release phase of the adaptive cycle there is expanded opportunity for novelty to succeed. Most people these days tend to think of novelty in purely technological terms, and it's true that email and Twitter can speed social change—for example, by helping organize an instant political rally. But spending hours each day alone in front of a screen does not necessarily lead to collaborative behavior, and it's just possible that we may not be able to count on our handheld devices continuing to function in the context of global economic crisis, trade disruptions, and resource shortages. Therefore perhaps it will be in our interactions within flesh-and-blood communities that our most decisive further innovations will arise.

The details are impossible to predict, but the general outline of our needed cooperative evolutionary leap is clear: we must develop a heightened collective ability to conserve natural resources while minimizing our human impacts on environmental systems. In some respects this might turn out to be little more than an updating of traditional societies' methods of managing common grazing or hunting lands. But today the stakes are far higher: the renewed commons must extend to include all renewable and nonrenewable resources, and "management" must bring extraction and harvest levels within the long-term ability of natural systems to recover and regenerate.

At the same time, with energy flows declining due to the depletion of fossil fuels, current levels of economic inequality will become unsupportable. Adaptation will require us to find ways of leveling the playing field peaceably.

Laying the groundwork for reorganization (following the release phase) will require building resilience into all our social structures and infrastructures. In the decades ahead, we must develop low-resource, low-energy ways of meeting human needs while nurturing an internalized imperative to keep population levels within ecosystems' long-term carrying capacity.

There are those who say that we humans are too selfish and individualistic to make this kind of evolutionary leap, and that even if it were possible there's simply too little time. If they're right, then this may be the end of the line: we might soon wind up in the "unfit" bin of evolutionary history. But given our spectacular history of cooperative achievement and our ability to transform our collective behavior rapidly via language (aided, for the time being, with instantaneous communications technology), it stands to reason that our species has at least a fair chance of making the cut.

To be sure, evolution will be driven by crisis. We will adapt by necessity. In this release phase there will be enormous potential for violence. Remember, release is the phase of the cycle in which capital is destroyed—and currently there are towering piles of human, built, and financial capital waiting to topple. We have been set up to compete for shards and scraps. It's no wonder that so many who sense the precariousness of our current situation have opted to become "preppers" and survivalists. But things will go a lot better for us if, rather than stocking up on guns and canned goods, we spend our time getting to know our neighbors, learning how to facilitate effective meetings, or helping design resilient local food systems. Survival will depend on finding cooperative paths in which sacrifice is shared, the best of our collective achievements are preserved, and compassion is nurtured.

Darwin tells us we must evolve or die, and current circumstances bring that choice into stark relief. A lot of people evidently think that fitness and selfishness are the same. But we've gotten ourselves into our current fix *not* because we're too good at cooperating to achieve collective fitness, but rather because, in our success, we failed to take account of the finite and fragile nature of the natural systems that support us. It's true that individual initiative is important and that group-think can be stultifying. Yet it is our ability to innovate socially and cooperate to increase our collective fitness that has gotten us this far, and that will determine whether we survive, and under what conditions, as we adapt to scarcity and reintegrate ourselves within ecosystems in the decades ahead.

— AUGUST 2012

▶ WANT TO CHANGE THE WORLD?
READ THIS FIRST

ISTORY IS OFTEN MADE BY STRONG PERSONALITIES WIELDING bold new political, economic, or religious doctrines. Yet any serious effort to understand how and why societies change requires examination not just of leaders and ideas, but also of environmental circumstances. The ecological context (climate, weather, and the presence or absence of water, good soil, and other resources) may either present or foreclose opportunities for those wanting to shake up the social world. This suggests that if you want to change society—or are interested in aiding or evaluating the efforts of others to do so—some understanding of exactly how environmental circumstances affect such efforts could be extremely helpful.

Perhaps the most important key to grasping the relationship between the environment and processes of societal change was articulated by American anthropologist Marvin Harris (1927–2001). From the very beginning of efforts to systematically study human societies in the 18th and 19th centuries, it had been clear that there were strong correlations between how societies obtain their food (whether by hunting and gathering, horticulture, agriculture, animal herding, or fishing), and their social structures and beliefs about the world. Hunter-gatherers typically live in small peripatetic bands, have an egalitarian social structure, and regard the natural world as full of supernatural powers and personalities that can be contacted or influenced by shamans. Farmers, on the other hand, stay in one place and produce seasonal surpluses that often end up subsidizing the formation of towns as well as classes of full-time specialists in various activities (metalworking, statecraft, soldiery, banking, recordkeeping, and so on); agricultural societies also tend to develop formalized religions presided over by a full-time, hierarchical priestly class. These systemic distinctions and similarities have held true on different continents and throughout centuries. Harris showed how shifts from one kind of food system to another were driven by environmental opportunity and necessity, and he refined his insights into an anthropological research strategy.[1]

Marvin Harris's magnum opus was the rather difficult book *Cultural Materialism: The Struggle for a Science of Culture* (1979).[2] While he was perfectly capable of writing for the general public—others of his titles, such as *Cows, Pigs, Wars and Witches* (1974) and *Cannibals and Kings* (1977) were best sellers—in *Cultural Materialism*, Harris was writing for fellow anthropologists. He uses a lot of technical jargon and argues each point meticulously, presenting a surfeit of evidence. However, the kernel of Harris's theoretical contribution can be summarized rather briefly.

All human societies consist of three interrelated spheres: first, the *infrastructure*, which comprises a society's relations to its environment, including its modes of production and reproduction—think of this primarily as its ways of getting food, energy, and materials; second, the *structure*, which comprises a society's economic, political, and social relations; and third, the *superstructure*, a society's symbolic and ideational aspects, including its religions, arts, rituals, sports and games, and science. Inevitably, these three spheres overlap, but they are also distinct, and it is literally impossible to find a human society that does not feature all three in some permutation.

For social change advocates, it's what comes next that should agitate the neurons. Harris's "cultural materialism"[3] argues for the principle of what he calls "probabilistic infrastructural determinism." That is to say, the structure and superstructure of societies are always contested to one degree or another. Battles over distribution of wealth and ideas are perennial and can have important consequences: life in the former East Germany was very different from life in West Germany, even though both were industrial nations operating under (what started out to be) nearly identical ecological conditions. However, *truly radical societal change tends to be associated with shifts of infrastructure.* When the basic relationship between a society and its ecosystem alters, people must reconfigure their political systems, economies, and ideology accordingly, even if they were perfectly happy with the previous state of affairs.

Societies change their infrastructure out of necessity (for example, due to depletion of resources) or opportunity (usually the increased availability of resources, made available perhaps by migration to new territory or by the adoption of a new technology). The Agricultural Revolution ten thousand years ago involved a massive infrastructural shift, and the fossil-fueled Industrial Revolution two hundred years ago had an even greater and far more rapid impact. In both cases, population levels grew, political and economic relations evolved, and ideas about the world mutated profoundly.

Explaining the former example in a bit more detail may help illustrate the concept. Harris was an early adopter of the now-common view of the Agricultural Revolution as an adaptive response to environmental shifts at the end of the Pleistocene epoch, a period of dramatic climate change. Glaciers were receding and species (especially big herbivorous prey animals such as mammoths and mastodons) faced extinction, with human predation hurrying that extinction process along. "In all centers of early agricultural activity," writes Harris,

> the end of the Pleistocene saw a notable broadening of the subsistence base to include more small mammals, reptiles, birds, mollusks, and insects. Such 'broad spectrum' systems were a symptom of hard times. As the labor costs of the

hunter-gatherer subsistence systems rose, and as the benefits fell, alternative sedentary modes of production became more attractive.

Lifestyles based on cultivation took root and spread, and with them (eventually) came villages and chiefdoms. In certain places, the latter in turn mutated to produce the most radical social invention of all, the state:

> The paleotechnic infrastructures most amendable to intensification, redistribution, and the expansion of managerial functions were those based on the grain and ruminant complexes of the Near and Middle East, southern Europe, northern China, and northern India. Unfortunately these were precisely the first systems to cross the threshold into statehood, and they therefore have never been directly observed by historians or ethnologists. [That is, no historians or ethnologists were around to witness these one-time-only events.] Nonetheless, from the archaeological evidence of storehouses, monumental architecture, temples, high mounds and tells, defensive moats, walls, towers, and the growth of irrigation systems, it is clear that managerial activities similar to those observed among surviving pre-state chiefdoms underwent rapid expansion in these critical regions immediately prior to the appearance of the state. Furthermore, there is abundant evidence from Roman encounters with "barbarians" in northern Europe, from Hebraic and Indian scriptures, and from Norse, Germanic, and Celtic sagas that intensifier-redistributor-warriors and their priestly retainers constituted the nuclei of the first ruling classes in the Old World.

While I have omitted most of Harris's detailed explanation, nevertheless we have here, in essence, an ecological explanation for the origin of civilization. What's more, Harris is not merely proposing an entertaining "just-so" story, but a scientific hypothesis that can be tested within the limits of available evidence.

Cultural materialism is capable of illuminating not just grand societal shifts, such as the origin of agriculture or the state, but the deeper functions of cultural institutions and practices of many sorts. Harris's excellent textbook *Cultural Anthropology* (2000, 2007),[4] coauthored with Orna Johnson, includes chapters with titles such as "Reproduction," "Economic Organization," "Domestic Life," and "Class and Caste"; each features illustrative sidebars showing how a relevant cultural practice (peacemaking among the Mehinacu of central Brazil, polyandry among the Nyimba of Nepal) is adaptive to environmental necessity. Throughout this and all his books, indeed throughout his entire career, Harris aimed to show that probabilistic infrastructural determinism is the only sound basis for a true "science of culture" capable of producing testable hypotheses to explain why societies evolve the way they do.

Why is this important now? For the simple reason that our own society is on the cusp of an enormous infrastructural transformation.

Which is remarkable, because we're still reeling from the previous one, which began just a couple of centuries ago. The fossil-fueled Industrial Revolution entailed a shift from reliance on mostly renewable energy sources—firewood, field crops, some water power, wind for sails, and animal muscle for traction—to cheaper, more controllable, more energy dense, and (in the case of oil) more portable nonrenewable sources.

Oil has given us the ability to dramatically increase the rate at which we extract and transform Earth's bounty (via mining machinery, tractors, and powered fishing boats), as well as the ability to transport people and materials at high speed and little cost. It and the other fossil fuels have also served as feedstocks for greatly expanded chemical and pharmaceutical industries, and have enabled a dramatic intensification of agricultural production while reducing the need for field labor. The results of fossil-fueling our infrastructure have included rapid population growth, the ballooning of the middle class, unprecedented levels of urbanization, and the construction of a consumer economy. While elements of the Scientific Revolution were in place a couple of centuries prior to our adoption of fossil fuels, cheap fossil energy supplied a means of vastly expanding scientific research and applying it to the development of a broad range of technologies that are themselves directly or indirectly fossil-fueled. With heightened mobility, immigration increased greatly, and the democratic multi-ethnic nation state became the era's emblematic political institution. As economies expanded almost continually due to the abundant availability of high-quality energy, neoliberal economic theory emerged as the world's primary ideology of societal management. It soon evolved to incorporate several unchallenged though logically unsupportable notions, including the belief that economies can grow forever and the assumption that the entire natural world is merely a subset of the human economy.

Now, however, our still-new infrastructural regime based on fossil fuels is already showing signs of winding down. There are two main reasons. One is climate change: carbon dioxide, produced in the burning of fossil fuels, is creating a greenhouse effect that is warming the planet. The consequences will be somewhere between severe and cataclysmic. If we continue burning fossil fuels, we're more likely to see a cataclysmic result, which could make continuation of industrial agriculture, and perhaps civilization itself, problematic. We do have the option to dramatically curtail fossil fuel consumption to avert catastrophic climate change. Either way, our current infrastructure will be a casualty.

The second big reason our fossil fuel-based infrastructure is endangered has to do with depletion. We're not running out of coal, oil, or natural gas in the absolute sense, but we have extracted these nonrenewable resources using the best-first, or low-hanging fruit, principle. With oil, the most strategically important of the fossil fuels (because of its centrality to transportation systems), we have already reached the point of diminishing returns. Compared to a decade ago, the global petroleum industry has more than doubled its rate of investment in exploration and production, while actual rates of global crude oil production have flatlined. Costs of production are rising, and drillers are targeting geological formations that were formerly considered too problematic to bother with. With oil, the fate of the world's economy appears to hang on the outcome of a race between technology and depletion: while industry spokespeople and media pundits tend to cheer new technology such as hydraulic fracturing ("fracking"), persistently high oil prices and soaring production costs suggest that depletion is in fact pulling ahead.[5] Coal and natural gas production will likely encounter similar diminishing-return limits within the next decade, both in the United States and worldwide.[6]

At a bare minimum, climate change and fossil fuel depletion will force society to change to different energy sources, giving up reliance on energy-dense and controllable coal, oil, and gas in favor of more diffuse and intermittent renewable sources like wind and solar. This in itself is likely to have enormous societal implications. While electric passenger cars running on power supplied by wind turbines and solar panels are feasible, electric airliners, container ships, and eighteen-wheel trucks are not. Distributed electricity generation from renewables, together with a decline in global shipping and air transport, may favor less globalized and more localized patterns of economic and political organization.

However, we must also consider the strong likelihood that our looming, inevitable shift away from fossil fuels will entail a substantial reduction in the amount of useful energy available to society. Wind and sunlight are abundant and free, but the technology used to capture energy from these ambient sources is made from nonrenewable minerals and metals. The mining, manufacturing, and transport activities necessary for the production and installation of wind turbines and solar panels currently require oil. It may theoretically be possible to replace oil with electricity from renewables in at least some of these processes, but for the foreseeable future wind and solar technologies can best be thought of as fossil fuel extenders.

Nuclear power, with its unbreakable reliance on mining and transport, is likewise a fossil fuel extender—but a far more dangerous one, given unsolved problems with accidents, nuclear proliferation, and waste storage. When the construction and decommissioning of power plants and the mining and processing of uranium are all taken into account, nuclear power also offers a relatively low energy return on the energy invested (EROEI) in producing it.[7]

Relatively low energy returns-on-investment from both nuclear and renewable energy sources may themselves result in societal change. The EROEI of fossil fuels was extremely high in comparison with that of energy sources previously available. This was a major factor in reducing the need for agricultural field labor, which in turn drove urbanization and the growth of the middle class. Some renewable sources of energy offer a better EROEI than firewood or agricultural crops, but none can compare with coal, oil, and gas in their heyday. This suggests that the social consequences of the end of cheap fossil energy may include a partial re-ruralization of society and a shrinking of the middle class (the latter process is already beginning in the United States).

With less useful energy available, the global economy will fail to grow, and will likely enter a sustained period of contraction. Increased energy efficiency may cushion the impact but cannot avert it. With economies no longer growing, our current globally dominant neo-liberal political-economic ideology may increasingly be called into question and eventually overthrown.

While energy is key to society's infrastructure, other factors require consideration as well. Fossil fuels are depleting, but so are a host of additional important resources, including metals, minerals, topsoil, and water. So far, we have made up for depletion in these cases by investing more energy in mining lower grade ores, by replacing soil nutrients with commercial fertilizers (many made from fossil fuels), and by transporting water, food, and other goods from places of local abundance to regions in which those materials are scarce. This strategy has increased the human carrying capacity of our planet but may not work much longer as energy itself becomes scarcer.

Further alterations in the links between the environment and society will arise from climate change. Even assuming that nations undertake dramatic reductions in carbon emissions soon, cumulative past emissions virtually guarantee continued and increasing impacts that will include rising sea levels and worsening droughts and floods. By midcentury, hundreds of millions of climate refugees may be in search of secure habitat.

There are optimistic ways of viewing the future, based on assumptions that fossil fuels are in fact abundant and will last another century or more, that new nuclear power technologies will be more viable than current ones, that renewable energy sources can be scaled up quickly, and that likely impacts of climate change have been overestimated. Even if one or more of these assumptions turns out to be correct, however, the evidence of declining returns on energy and financial investments in oil extraction cannot be disregarded. An infrastructure shift is underway. Considering oil's role in industrial agriculture,[8] this shift will undoubtedly and profoundly impact our food system—and food (which is our most basic energy source, from a biological perspective) is at the core of every society's infrastructure. Whether or not optimistic assumptions are valid, we probably face an infrastructural transformation at least as significant as the Industrial Revolution.

But the error bars on energy supplies and climate sensitivity include more pessimistic possibilities. A faltering of useful fossil energy supply rates could trigger an unwinding of the global financial system as well as international conflict. It is also possible that the relationship between carbon emissions and atmospheric temperatures is nonlinear, with Earth's climate system subject to self-reinforcing feedbacks that could result in a massive die-off of species, our own included.

Choose your assumptions—optimistic, pessimistic, or somewhere in between. In any case, this is a big deal.

We are living at a historic moment when the structure of society (economic and political systems) and its superstructure (ideologies) are about to be challenged as never before. When infrastructure changes, what seemingly was solid melts into air, paradigms fall, and institutions crumble, until a new societal regime emerges. Think of a caterpillar pupating, its organ systems evidently being reduced to undifferentiated protoplasm before reorganizing themselves into the features of a butterfly. What a perfect opportunity for an idealist intent on changing the world!

Indeed, fault lines are already appearing throughout society. From a cultural materialist point of view, the most important of these relate to *how* the inevitable infrastructure change will occur. Proponents of distributed renewable energy sources are the underdogs while the defenders of centralized, fossil energy systems the incumbents in deepening disputes over subsidies and other elements of government energy policy. Meanwhile, grassroots opposition to extreme fossil fuel extraction methods is springing up everywhere that companies are fracking for oil and gas, drilling in deep water, mining tar sands, or blasting mountaintops to mine coal. Opposition to an oil pipeline is fueling one of the hottest political fires in Washington, DC. And concern about climate change has acquired an intergenerational dimension, as young people across America sue state governments and federal agencies for failing to develop climate action plans.[9] Young people, after all, are the ones who will most forcibly face the consequences of climate change, and their attitude toward older generations may not be forgiving.[10]

We are also seeing increasing conflict over the structure of society—its systems of economic distribution and political decision-making. As economic growth grinds to a halt, the world's wealthy investor class is seeking to guarantee its solvency and maintain its profits by shifting costs onto the general public via bailouts, austerity measures, and quantitative easing (which lowers interest rates, flushing money out of savings accounts and into the stock market). Jobs downsize and wages fall, but the number of billionaires billows. However, rising economic inequality has its own political costs, as documented in Amazon's recent best-selling book, a 700-page tome called *Capital in the Twenty-First Century*,[11] which unfortunately fails to grasp the infrastructural shift that is upon us or its implications for economy and society. Polls show rising dissatisfaction with political leaders and parties throughout the West. But in most countries there is no organized opposition group poised to take advantage of this widespread discontent. Instead, political and economic institutions are themselves losing legitimacy.[12]

Infrastructural tremors are also reverberating throughout international geopolitics. The world's dominant superpower, which attained its status during the 20th century at least partly because it was the home of the global oil industry, is now quickly losing diplomatic clout and military "credibility" as the result of a series of disastrous miscalculations and blunders, including its invasions and occupations of Afghanistan and Iraq. Coal-fueled China is just now becoming the world's largest economy,[13] though it and other second-tier nations (UK, Germany, Russia) are themselves beset with intractable and growing economic contradictions, pollution dilemmas, and resource limits.[14]

Society's superstructure is also subject to deepening rupture, with neoliberalism coming under increasing criticism, especially since 2008. However, there is a more subtle and pervasive (and therefore potentially even more potent) superstructure to modern society, one largely taken for granted and seldom named or discussed, and it is likewise under assault. Essayist John Michael Greer calls this "the civil religion of progress."[15] As Greer has written, the idea of progress has quietly become the central article of faith of the modern industrial world, more universally held than the doctrine of any organized religion. The notion that "history has a direction, and it has to make cumulative progress in that direction" has been common to both capitalist and communist societies during the past century.[16] But what will happen to that "religious" conviction as the economy shrinks, technology fails, population declines, and inventors fail to come up with ways of managing society's multiplying crises? More to the point, how will billions of fragile human psyches adjust to seeing their most cherished creed battered repeatedly upon the shoals of reality? And what new faith will replace it? Greer suggests that it will be one that reconnects humanity with nature, though its exact form is yet to reveal itself.[17]

All of these trends are in their very earliest phases. As infrastructure actually shifts—as fuels deplete, as weather extremes worsen—tiny cracks in the edifice of business-as-usual will become unbridgeable chasms.

Here's my last big takeaway message for would-be social changers: Only ideas, demonstration projects, and policy proposals that fit our emerging infrastructure will have genuine usefulness or staying power. How can you know if your idea fits the emerging infrastructure? There's no hard and fast rule, but your idea stands a good chance if it assumes we are moving toward a societal regime with less energy and less transport (and that is therefore more localized); if it can work in a world where climate is changing and weather conditions are extreme and unpredictable; if it provides a way to sequester carbon rather than releasing more into the atmosphere; and if it helps people meet their basic needs during hard times.

It's fairly easy to identify elements of our society's existing structure and superstructure that *won't* work with the infrastructure toward which we appear to be headed. Consumerism and corporatism are two big ones; these were 20th-century adaptations to cheap, abundant energy. They justifiably have been the objects of a great deal of activist opposition in recent decades. There were reforms or alternatives to consumerism and corporatism that *could have worked* within our industrial infrastructure regime (or that did work in some places, not others): European-style industrial socialism is the primary example, though that might be thought of as a magnetic hub for a host of idealistic proposals championed by thousands, maybe even millions of would-be world-changers. But industrial socialism is arguably just as thoroughly dependent on fossil-fueled infrastructure as corporatism and consumerism. To the extent that it is, activists who are married to an industrial-socialist vision of an ideal world may be wasting many of their efforts needlessly.

Historic examples offer useful ways of grounding social proposals. In the current context, it is important to remember that almost all of human history took place in a preindustrial, "pre-progress" context, so it should be fairly easy to differentiate desirable from undesirable societal adaptations to analogous challenges in past eras. For example, anarchist philosopher and evolutionary biologist Peter Kropotkin, in his book *Mutual Aid*, praised medieval European cities as sites of autonomy and creativity—though the period during which they flourished is often thought of as a "dark age."

There are plenty of activist projects underway now that appear thoroughly aligned with the post-fossil fuel infrastructure toward which we are headed, including permaculture cooperatives, eco-villages, local food campaigns, and Transition Initiatives. Relevant new economic trends include the collaborative economy, the sharing economy, collaborative consumption, distributed production, P2P finance, and the open source and open knowledge movements.[18] While some of the latter merely constitute new business models that appear to spring from Web-based technologies and social media, their attractiveness may partly derive from a broadly shared cultural sense that the centralized systems of production and consumption characteristic of the 20th century are simply no longer viable, and must give way to more horizontal, distributed networks. The list of existing ideas and projects that could help society adapt in a post-fossil fuel era is long. Plenty of people have sensed the direction of global change and come to their own sensible conclusions about what to do, without any awareness of Harris's cultural materialism.

But such awareness could help at the margins by reducing wasted effort.

Do you want to change the world? More power to you. Start by identifying your core values—fairness, peace, stability, beauty, resilience, whatever. That's up to you. Figure out what ideas, projects, proposals, or policies further those values, but also fit with the infrastructure that's almost certainly headed our way. Then get to work. There's plenty to do, and lots at stake.

— JUNE 2014

Notes

Chapter 1: Ten Years After

1. scientificamerican.com/article/the-end-of-cheap-oil/. The full article can be found at oilcrisis.com/campbell/endofcheapoil.pdf
2. resilience.org/stories/2004-05-11/dick-cheney-peak-oil-and-final-count-down
3. communitysolution.org/04conf.html
4. peakoil.net/conferences/iwood-2004-berlin
5. See youtube.com/watch?v=cJ-J9iSwP8w
6. postcarbon.org/drill-baby-drill/report
7. forbes.com/sites/modeledbehavior/2013/07/17/no-peak-oil-really-is-dead
8. postcarbon.org/drill-baby-drill/report
9. nytimes.com/2010/02/15/business/energy-environment/15renoil.html
10. advisorperspectives.com/dshort/updates/DOT-Miles-Driven.php
11. theoildrum.com/node/3487. The images at that post are now broken links, but the critical chart can be seen here: theoildrum.com/files/StuartFig2.jpg
12. cassandralegacy.blogspot.it/2013/08/who-said-that-peak-oil-models-were-wrong.html
13. youtube.com/watch?v=D9z1Ikn84Aw
14. theoildrum.com/node/9946
15. resilience.org/stories/2006-07-06/open-letter-greg-palast
16. See en.wikipedia.org/wiki/Uppsala_Protocol and richardheinberg.com/odp

Chapter 2: The Gross Society

1. en.wikipedia.org/wiki/Boom_Town_%28film%29
2. breakingenergy.com/2014/02/18/peak-oil-is-real-and-the-majors-face-challenging-times
3. postcarbon.org/drill-baby-drill/report

4. csmonitor.com/Environment/Energy-Voices/2013/0702/Why-oil
-and-gas-drilling-is-going-deeper-and-further-offshore

5. bloomberg.com/news/2014-02-27/dream-of-u-s-oil-independence
-slams-against-shale-costs.html

6. energypolicy.columbia.edu/events-calendar/global-oil-market-forecast
ing-main-approaches-key-drivers

7. reuters.com/article/2014/02/17/oil-exploration-spending-idUSL3N0L
J38A20140217

8. peakoilmatters.com/2014/02/06/peak-oil-investment-issues-3

9. energypolicy.columbia.edu/events-calendar/global-oil-market-forecast
ing-main-approaches-key-drivers

10. economist.com/node/17314626?subjectid=2512631&story_id=17314626

11. ftalphaville.ft.com/files/2013/01/Perfect-Storm-LR.pdf

12. mdpi.com/2071-1050/3/10/1796/pdf

13. mdpi.com/2071-1050/3/10/1796/pdf

14. mdpi.com/1996-1073/2/1/25/pdf

15. ourfiniteworld.com/2014/02/25/beginning-of-the-end-oil-companies
-cut-back-on-spending

16. people.hofstra.edu/geotrans/eng/ch3en/conc3en/vehiclemilesusa.html

17. usatoday.com/story/news/nation/2013/10/01/social-media-driving
-millennials/2898093

18. washingtonpost.com/blogs/wonkblog/wp/2013/12/13/cars-in-the-u-s
-are-more-fuel-efficient-than-ever-heres-how-it-happened

19. ourfiniteworld.com/2013/01/31/why-is-us-oil-consumption-lower
-better-gasoline-mileage

20. See postcarbon.org/report/127153-energy-nine-challenges-of
-alternative-energy

21. nationofchange.org/need-jobs-us-solar-industry-provides-employment
-more-people-coal-and-oil-combined-1391783404

22. bls.gov/news.release/archives/empsit_05022014.htm

23. zerohedge.com/news/2014-01-10/people-not-labor-force-soar-record
-918-million-participation-rate-plunges-1978-level

24. gallup.com/poll/166850/americans-worse-off-financially-year-ago.aspx

25. resilience.org/stories/2012-03-05/uneconomic-growth-deepens
-depression

26. dailyreckoning.com/credit-growth-drives-economic-growth-until-it
-doesn%E2%80%99t

27. 2012wiki.com/index.php?title=Image:Diminishing_Returns_from
_Each_Dollar_of_New_Debt_in_US_Economy.jpg

28. reuters.com/article/2013/12/06/us-usa-qe3-piktoggles-special-report
-idUSBRE9B50G620131206

29. cnbc.com/id/101237862

30. huffingtonpost.com/2013/06/01/happiness-index-only-1-in_n_3354
524.html

31. dailymail.co.uk/news/article-1260329/Worlds-largest-cities-morphing
-overcrowded-mega-regions-defined-poverty-pollution-UN-report
-warns.html

32. thedailybeast.com/articles/2012/01/14/consumption-makes-us-sad
-science-says-we-can-be-happy-with-less.html

33. dancingrabbit.org

34. resilience.org/stories/2014-02-11/medieval-spanish-ghost-town-now
-self-sufficient-ecovillage

35. transitionnetwork.org

36. See "The Purposefully Confusing World of Energy Politics," Chapter 5
in this book.

Chapter 4: The Climate PR Puzzle

1. Arguably, overpopulation is as big an issue as our energy-climate
conundrum. I've chosen not to focus on it here merely to streamline the
narrative. There are many feedbacks between population, energy, and
climate, and these deserve discussion elsewhere.

2. ec.europa.eu/clima/policies/roadmap/faq_en.htm

3. sciencedirect.com/science/article/pii/S0301421510008645

4. amazon.com/The-Five-Stages-Collapse-Survivors/dp/0865717362/ref
=sr_1_1?ie=UTF8&qid=1383196999&sr=8-1&keywords=five+stages
+of+collapse

5. cluborlov.blogspot.com/2013/10/the-sixth-stage-of-collapse.html

6. Rogers, Everett M., *Diffusion of Innovations*, (Glencoe: Free Press, 1962).

7. sustainabilityinstitute.org/pubs/Leverage_Points.pdf

8. amazon.com/Voluntary-Simplicity-Toward-Outwardly-Inwardly/dp
/0061779261/ref=pd_sim_b_3

9. For more suggestions to elected officials, see this "top 10" list compiled
by Herman Daly: resilience.org/stories/2013-10-29/top-10-policies-for
-a-steady-state-economy

Chapter 5: The Purposely Confusing World of Energy Politics

1. articles.latimes.com/2013/jun/21/opinion/la-oe-zierman-california-fracking-moratorium-20130621

2. sourcewatch.org/index.php/Fracking_and_water_pollution

3. bloomberg.com/news/2014-01-04/study-shows-fracking-is-bad-for-babies.html

4. scientificamerican.com/article/a-path-to-sustainable-energy-by-2030

5. See greens.org/s-r/60/60-09.html, https://socialsciences.arts.unsw.edu.au/tsw/JandDreplytoreply.htm, and andrew.cmu.edu/user/pjaramil/ClIMA/Publications_files/Energy%20Policy%202013%20Gilbraith.pdf

6. See stanford.edu/group/efmh/jacobson/Articles/I/NYSWWSResp Comm.pdf and sciencedirect.com/science/article/pii/S0301421512009792

7. ourfiniteworld.com/2014/01/21/ten-reasons-intermittent-renewables-wind-and-solar-pv-are-a-problem

8. solavis.ch/files/Fossil_Infrastructure_Cost_vs_Renewable_Energy_System_Cost.pdf

9. amazon.com/Spains-Photovoltaic-Revolution-Investment-Springer Briefs/dp/144199436X

10. americanenergyindependence.com/solarenergy.aspx

11. sciencedirect.com/science/article/pii/S0301421511004836

12. nature.com/nclimate/journal/v3/n2/full/nclimate1683.html

13. oedigital.com/energy/shale/item/2810-ioc-production-falls-25-in-past-12-years

14. online.wsj.com/news/articles/SB10001424052702303277704579348332283819314

15. bloomberg.com/news/2014-01-30/shell-profit-drops-48-as-oil-and-gas-production-declines.html

16. postcarbon.org/drill-baby-drill/report

17. scientificamerican.com/article/climate-science-predictions-prove-too-conservative

18. climatedepot.com/2013/11/25/a-planned-economic-recession-global-warming-prof-kevin-anderson-who-has-cut-back-on-showering-to-save-planet-asserts-economic-de-growth-is-needed-continuing-with-ec/

19. greencarreports.com/news/1089555_electric-car-market-share-in-2013-understanding-the-numbers-better

Chapter 6: The Brief, Tragic Reign of Consumerism

1. powells.com/biblio/1-9780465021550-1
2. powells.com/biblio/61-9780465061792-1
3. powells.com/biblio/1-9780486280622-1
4. amazon.com/Living-Sanely-Simply-Troubled-World/dp/0805203001 /ref=sr_1_2?ie=UTF8&qid=1373417620&sr=8-2&keywords=living +the+good+life+nearing
5. amazon.com/Challenge-Mans-Future-Harrison-Brown/dp/0813300 339/ref=sr_1_1?ie=UTF8&qid=1373397503&sr=8-1&keywords=the +challenge+of+man%27s+future
6. amazon.com/Limits-Growth-Donella-H-Meadows/dp/0451057678 /ref=sr_1_2?ie=UTF8&qid=1373397682&sr=8-2&keywords=the +limits+to+growth
7. csiro.au/files/files/plje.pdf
8. en.wikipedia.org/wiki/Ecological_economics
9. spiegel.de/international/germany/peak-oil-and-the-german-govern ment-military-study-warns-of-a-potentially-drastic-oil-crisis-a-715138 .html, unep.org/newscentre/default.aspx?DocumentID=2697&Article ID=9303
10. grossnationalhappiness.com
11. happyplanetindex.org

Chapter 7: Fingers in the Dike

1. resilience.org/stories/2013-09-19/peak-oil-demand-peak-oil
2. peakoilbarrel.com/shocker-world-depending-usa-save-peak-oil
3. postcarbon.org/drill-baby-drill/report
4. latimes.com/business/la-fi-oil-20140521-story.html
5. huffingtonpost.com/2013/09/25/shell-abandons-oil-shale_n_3991716 .html
6. amazon.com/The-End-Growth-Adapting-Economic/dp/0865716951/ ref=sr_1_1?ie=UTF8&qid=1380303127&sr=8-1&keywords=heinberg +end+of+growth
7. https://medium.com/the-physics-arxiv-blog/5e1dd9d1642
8. elsa.berkeley.edu/~saez/saez-UStopincomes-2012.pdf
9. ellenbrown.com/2013/02/24/how-the-fed-could-fix-the-economy-and -why-it-hasnt
10. metoffice.gov.uk/research/news/recent-pause-in-warming

11. wattsupwiththat.com/2013/09/05/statistical-proof-of-the-pause-over estimated-global-warming-over-the-past-20-years

12. npr.org/2013/08/29/216415005/a-cooler-pacific-may-be-behind-recent -pause-in-global-warming

13. smh.com.au/environment/climate-change/global-warming-pause -caused-by-la-nina-20130829-2ss3p.html

14. resilience.org/stories/2013-09-26/faux-pause-ocean-warming-sea-level -rise-and-polar-ice-melt-speed-up-surface-warming-to-follow

15. news.bbc.co.uk/2/shared/bsp/hi/pdfs/27_09_13_ipccsummary.pdf

16. bbc.co.uk/news/science-environment-24173504

17. There are countless resources for all these ideas; some of the best can be found at resilience.org and transitionus.org

Chapter 9: The Fight of the Century

1. Joseph Tainter, *The Collapse of Complex Societies*, New York: Cambridge University Press, 1988.

2. Ibid., 23.

3. See, for example, George Soros's comments in this recent *Newsweek* interview: newsweek.com/george-soros-coming-us-class-war-64271

4. nybooks.com/blogs/nyrblog/2012/jan/06/europe-cutting-hope

5. huffingtonpost.com/pavlina-r-tcherneva/navigating-the-jobs-crisi_b _370387.html

6. energybulletin.net/stories/2012-01-27/why-climate-change-will-make -you-love-big-government

7. guardian.co.uk/commentisfree/cifamerica/2012/jan/19/ecuador-radical -exciting-place

8. As described by John Michael Greer in *The Ecotechnic Future*, powells .com/biblio/2-9780865716391-2, 70 ff.

9. See Michael Shuman, *The Small-Mart Revolution*, amazon.com/The -Small-Mart-Revolution-Businesses-Competition/dp/1576754669

10. powells.com/biblio/62-9781603583435-0

11. truth-out.org/occupy-neighborhood/1326472096

12. truth-out.org/what-happened-canada/1327935024

13. nytimes.com/2012/01/09/world/europe/amid-economic-strife-greeks -look-to-farming-past.html?_r=1

14. world-governance.org/spip.php?article469

15. powells.com/biblio/1-9780865716858-0

16. For an entertaining and quick summary of the French Revolution, its failures, and its consequences, see the vlogbrothers video series at youtube.com/watch?v=BvSod16wfgg

Chapter 10: The Anthropocene: It's *Not* All About Us

1. marklynas.org/2011/05/welcome-to-the-anthropocene
2. ericcavalcanti.wordpress.com/2011/02/08/the-anthropocene-and-the -new-green-stewart-brand-on-edge
3. amazon.com/Love-Your-Monsters-Postenvironmentalism-Anthropo cene-ebook/dp/B006FKUJY6
4. amazon.com/Rambunctious-Garden-Saving-Nature-Post-Wild/dp /160819454X/ref=sr_1_1?s=books&ie=UTF8&qid=1395765262&sr =1-1&keywords=marris
5. resilience.org/stories/2014-04-13/did-crude-oil-production-actually -peak-in-2005
6. worldwatch.org/nuclear-power-after-fukushima
7. enenews.com/pbs-reporter-the-whole-world-needs-to-pay-attention -to-whats-going-on-at-fukushima-magnitude-of-mess-is-actually -staggering-we-really-dont-know-how-theyre-going-to
8. en.wikipedia.org/wiki/High-level_radioactive_waste_management
9. online.wsj.com/news/articles/SB121055252677483933
10. forbes.com/sites/tomaspray/2011/07/26/uranium-shortage-cant-be -ignored
11. commondreams.org/headlines03/0427-02.htm
12. economist.com/node/21549936
13. powermag.com/blog/the-ups-and-downs-of-u-s-nuclear-power
14. imdb.com/title/tt1992193
15. beyondnuclear.org/pandoras-false-promises
16. scientificamerican.com/article.cfm?id=are-new-types-of-reactors -needed-for-nuclear-renaissance
17. rainforestconservation.org/rainforest-primer/3-rainforests-in-peril -deforestation/c-human-use-of-biological-productivity-the-diversion -of-net-primary-productivity
18. resilience.org/stories/2014-02-11/the-purposely-confusing-world-of -energy-politics
19. co-intelligence.org/P-permaculture.html
20. See permacultureprinciples.com

21. landinstitute.org

22. transitionnetwork.org

23. See the work of Population Media Center, populationmedia.org

24. en.wikipedia.org/wiki/Maximum_power_principle

25. theoildrum.com/node/2592

26. diva-portal.org/smash/get/diva2:235822/FULLTEXT01.pdf

27. monbiot.com/2014/03/24/destroyer-of-worlds

28. rsta.royalsocietypublishing.org/content/369/1938/1010.full

29. ecologyandsociety.org/vol16/iss2/art12

30. For a rather irreverent take on popular misconceptions about the "Dark Ages," see cracked.com/article_20615_5-ridiculous-myths-you-probably-believe-about-dark-ages.html

Chapter 11: Conflict in the Era of Economic Decline

1. See, for example, motherboard.vice.com/2012/9/10/we-are-now-one-year-and-counting-from-global-riots-complex-systems-theorists-say--2

2. resilience.org/stories/2012-11-08/the-post-american-future

3. carolmoore.net/nuclearwar/alternatescenarios.html

4. thewhitereview.org/interviews/interview-with-david-graeber

5. energybulletin.net/stories/2012-02-16/david-graeber-anthropologist-anarchist-financial-analyst

Chapter 12: All Roads Lead Local

1. pressdemocrat.com/article/20140525/business/140529729#page=0

2. latimes.com/business/la-fi-oil-20140521-story.html

3. scientificamerican.com/article/a-path-to-sustainable-energy-by-2030

4. theenergycollective.com/jared-anderson/382141/german-lesson-renewable-power-policies

5. kevinanderson.info/blog/avoiding-dangerous-climate-change-demands-de-growth-strategies-from-wealthier-nations

6. reuters.com/article/2012/11/14/us-usa-obama-climate-idUSBRE8AD1IU20121114

7. transitionus.org

8. ilsr.org/key-studies-walmart-and-bigbox-retail

Chapter 13: Our Evanescent Culture

1. bloomberg.com/apps/news?pid=newsarchive&sid=aJfoZOXN22jY

2. en.wikipedia.org/wiki/Decline_of_newspapers

3. publishersweekly.com/pw/by-topic/industry-news/financial-reporting /article/61667-book-sales-rose-1-in-2013.html. beyondthemargins.com /2013/06/book-facts-and-stats

4. However, it should be noted that vinyl is making a strong niche comeback; see nytimes.com/2013/06/10/arts/music/vinyl-records-are -making-a-comeback.html?pagewanted=all&_r=0

5. libraryjournal.com/article/CA6574501.html

6. en.wikipedia.org/wiki/Media_preservation. See also theatlantic.com/ technology/archive/2014/05/the-library-of-congress-wants-to-destroy -your-old-cds-for-science/370804

7. postcarbon.org/report/44377-searching-for-a-miracle

8. spectrum.ieee.org/energy/the-smarter-grid/a-perfect-storm-of -planetary-proportions

9. pakistaniat.com/2009/01/06/electricity-crisis-in-pakistan

10. telegraph.co.uk/finance/newsbysector/energy/oilandgas/6142972 /Britain-heading-back-to-the-dark-ages.html

11. news.bbc.co.uk/2/hi/science/nature/8249540.stm

Chapter 14: Our Cooperative Darwinian Moment

1. dailymail.co.uk/sciencetech/article-1317867/Prehistoric-humans -compassion-cared-others.html

2. amazon.com/Overshoot-Ecological-Basis-Revolutionary-Change/dp /0252009886

3. jayhanson.us/_Systems/PopulationCrash_ProspectsForFamineInThe Twenty-FirstCentury.pdf

4. resalliance.org/index.php/key_concepts

5. powells.com/biblio/61-9781441522245-1

6. phys.org/news/2012-07-cooperation-trump-competition-monkeys.html

7. dailymail.co.uk/news/article-533571/Animal-magic-Why-species -helping-hand-flipper.html

8. fulltextarchive.com/pdfs/Mutual-Aid.pdf

9. nytimes.com/2009/08/21/books/21book.html?pagewanted=all

10. plosone.org/article/info%3Adoi%2F10.1371%2Fjournal.pone.0026922

11. alternet.org/belief/us-vs-them-simple-recipe-prevent-strong-society -forming

12. amazon.com/Energy-Equity-Ideas-Progress-Illich/dp/0714510580/ref =sr_1_1?ie=UTF8&qid=1343933288&sr=8-1&keywords=ivan+illich +energy+and+equity

Chapter 15: Want to Change the World? Read This First

1. The simple observation that human culture is adaptive to environmental conditions is revelatory: Jared Diamond (author of *Guns, Germs and Steel*) has based a career on it, though he consistently fails to credit Harris—who was earlier and more thorough. Harris himself was careful to cite predecessors upon whose work he was building, including Karl Marx.

2. books.google.com/books?id=8Xc9DMbB5KQC&printsec=frontcover &dq=%22materialism%22&hl=en&ei=meSKTIetFMu8cZOwyMkE &sa=X&oi=book_result&ct=result&resnum=10&ved=0CFUQ6AE wCQ#v=onepage&q&f=false

3. The term *materialism* is loaded with connotations that distract from the issues at hand. Marvin Harris uses it to refer merely to a way of thinking that assumes material effects are due to material causes. When I was teaching a college program on sustainability, I suggested to my students that they think of probabilistic infrastructural determinism as "cultural ecology." I knew this was somewhat inaccurate, as cultural ecology is a school of anthropological thought (en.wikipedia.org/wiki/Cultural _ecology) closely related to, but distinct from, cultural materialism. However, many students simply couldn't get past the word *materialism*: for them, this was an irremediably distasteful term associated both with the negation of spirituality and with the American mania for buying and consuming corporate products.

4. amazon.com/Cultural-Anthropology-Marvin-Harris/dp/0205454437 /ref=sr_1_1?ie=UTF8&qid=1399841320&sr=8-1&keywords=marvin +harris+cultural+anthropology

5. See the essay "The Gross Society," Chapter 2 in this book.

6. amazon.com/Blackout-Coal-Climate-Energy-Crisis/dp/0865716560 /ref=sr_1_1?ie=UTF8&qid=1399308687&sr=8-1&keywords=black out+heinberg

7. scientificamerican.com/article/eroi-behind-numbers-energy-return -investment/

8. postcarbon.org/report/41306-the-food-and-farming-transition-toward

9. america.aljazeera.com/articles/2014/5/4/youth-sue-governmentfor climateinaction.html

10. theglobeandmail.com/life/health-and-fitness/health/youth-anxiety-on -the-rise-amid-changing-climate/article18372258/

11. amazon.com/Capital-Twenty-First-Century-Thomas-Piketty/dp/067
443000X/ref=sr_1_1?ie=UTF8&qid=1399480770&sr=8-1&keywords
=piketty
12. gallup.com/poll/5392/trust-government.aspx
13. bloomberg.com/news/2014-04-30/china-set-to-overtake-u-s-as
-biggest-economy-using-ppp-measure.html
14. postcarbon.org/article/941201-end-of-growth-update-neither-a
15. thearchdruidreport.blogspot.com/2013/04/the-religion-of-progress
.html
16. resilience.org/stories/2013-09-18/life-preservers-for-mermaids
17. resilience.org/stories/2013-09-18/life-preservers-for-mermaids
18. resilience.org/stories/2014-05-05/the-sharing-economy-capitalism-s
-last-stand

Index

About the Author

RICHARD HEINBERG is Senior Fellow of Post Carbon Institute and author of 11 previous books, including *The Party's Over, Powerdown, Peak Everything, The End of Growth,* and *Snake Oil.* His essays appear on websites Resilience.org and Commondreams.org, as well as *Solutions Journal.* During the past decade-and-a-half he has given hundreds of lectures on energy and the environment to audiences around the world. He is also an avid amateur violinist and, together with his wife Janet Barocco, lives in a suburban permaculture home with chickens, fruit and nut trees, and herb and vegetable gardens.

If you have enjoyed *Afterburn*, you might also enjoy other

BOOKS TO BUILD A NEW SOCIETY

Our books provide positive solutions for people who want to make a difference. We specialize in:

Food & Gardening ◆ Resilience ◆ Sustainable Building
Climate Change ◆ Energy ◆ Health & Wellness
Sustainable Living ◆ Environment & Economy
Progressive Leadership ◆ Community
Educational & Parenting Resources

For a full list of NSP's titles, please call 1-800-567-6772 *or check out our web site at:*

www.newsociety.com